P9-EAY-562

SECOND EDITION

Cite Right

A Quick Guide to Citation Styles— MLA, APA, Chicago, the Sciences, Professions, and More

Charles Lipson

The University of Chicago Press CHICAGO AND LONDON

Charles Lipson is the Peter B. Ritzma Professor and director of undergraduate studies in political science at the University of Chicago.

The University of Chicago Press, Chicago 60637
The University of Chicago Press, Ltd., London

© 2006, 2011 by Charles Lipson
All rights reserved. Published 2011.
Printed in the United States of America

20 19 18 17 16 15 14 13   2 3 4 5

ISBN-13: 978-0-226-48463-1 (cloth)
ISBN-10: 0-226-48463-7 (cloth)
ISBN-13: 978-0-226-48464-8 (paper)
ISBN-10: 0-226-48464-5 (paper)

Library of Congress Cataloging-in-Publication Data

Lipson, Charles.
    Cite right: a quick guide to citation styles—MLA, APA, Chicago, the sciences, professions, and more / Charles Lipson. — 2nd ed.
        p. cm. — (Chicago guides to writing, editing, and publishing)
    Includes index.
    ISBN-13: 978-0-226-48463-1 (cloth: alk. paper)
    ISBN-10: 0-226-48463-7 (cloth: alk. paper)
    ISBN-13: 978-0-226-48464-8 (pbk.: alk. paper)
    ISBN-10: 0-226-48464-5 (pbk.: alk. paper)
    1. Bibliographical citations. I. Title. II. Series: Chicago guides to writing, editing, and publishing.
    PN171.F56L55 2011
    808'.027—dc22   2010024721

⊗ This paper meets the requirements of ANSI/NISO Z39.48-1992 (Permanence of Paper).

Cite Right

Chicago Guides
to *Writing*, *Editing*,
and Publishing

To my students,

who have made

teaching so rewarding

CONTENTS

Citations: An Overview

1 WHY CITE?

There are three reasons to cite the materials you use:

- To give credit to others' work and ideas, whether you agree with them or not. When you use their words, you must give them credit by using both quotation marks and citations.
- To show readers the materials on which you base your analysis, your narrative, or your conclusions.
- To guide readers to the materials you have used so they can examine it for themselves. Their interest might be to confirm your work, to challenge it, or simply to explore it further.

Taken together, these citations fully disclose your sources. That's important for academic integrity in several ways.

First, good citations parcel out credit. Some belongs to you for the original work you did; you need to take full responsibility for it. Some belongs to others for their words, ideas, data, drawings, or other work. You need to acknowledge it, openly and explicitly.

Second, if you relied on others' work in order to tell your story, explain your topic, or document your conclusions, you need to say exactly what you used. Take a sample paper about World War I. No one writing today learned about it firsthand. What we know, we learned by reading books and articles, by examining original documents and news reports, by listening to oral histories, by reviewing data compiled by military historians, and perhaps by viewing photographs or movies. When we write about the war, then, we should say how we acquired our information. The only exception is "commonly known information," something that everyone in the field clearly understands and that does not require any substantiation.[1] There's no need for a footnote to prove Woodrow Wilson was actually president of the United States. But if you referred to his speech declaring war, you would need a proper citation. If you used his words, you'd need quotation marks, too.

Third, your readers may want to pursue a particular issue you covered.

---

1. What counts as common knowledge depends on your audience.

Citations should lead them to the right sources, whether those are books, interviews, archival documents, websites, poems, or paintings. That guidance serves several purposes. Skeptical readers may doubt the basis for your work or your conclusions. Others may simply want to double-check them or do more research on the topic. Your citations should point the way.

What citations should *not* do is prance about, showing off your knowledge without adding to the reader's. That's just bragging.

Beyond this question of style (and good manners), there is the basic issue of honesty. *Citations should never mislead your readers.* There are lots of ways to mislead or misdirect your readers; accurate citations avoid them. For example, they should not imply you read books or articles when you really didn't. They should not imply you spent days in the archives deciphering original documents when you actually read them in an edited book or, worse, when you "borrowed" the citation from a scholar who *did* study the originals. Of course, it's fine to cite that author or an edited collection. That's accurate. It's fine to burrow into the archives and read the original yourself. It's dishonest, though, to write citations that only pretend you did.

Good citations should reveal your sources, not conceal them. They should honestly show the research you conducted. That means they should give credit where credit is due, disclose the materials on which you base your work, and guide readers to that material so they can explore it further. Citations like those accurately reflect your work and that of others. They show the ground on which you stand.

WHICH CITATION FORMAT SHOULD YOU USE?

With so many formats available, which one should you choose?

The answer is usually straightforward: most fields rely on one format. In English literature, for instance, most papers and articles use MLA. In chemistry, they use ACS. A few fields use two styles, depending on the journal or publisher. Mathematics has a couple of citation styles, both of them unique to that field. Political science also uses two styles: APA for journals that prefer in-text citations and Chicago for journals that prefer true footnotes or endnotes. All these styles, and many more, are included in the chapters that follow.

Cite Right labels each chapter so you can see which fields use which style. If you are still unsure, you can find the answer in a couple of ways. If you're a student, simply ask your professor or teaching assistant. If you're writing for publication in a journal, review that journal's recent articles and its instructions for authors, either in the journal itself or on its website. Even if you don't plan on getting published, it's a good idea to look at the leading journals in your field and follow their style.

2 THE BASICS OF CITATION

Acknowledging your sources is crucial to doing honest academic work. That means citing them properly, using one of several styles. The one you choose depends on your field, your professor's advice if you are a student, and your own preferences.

There are three major citation styles:

- Chicago (or Turabian), used in many fields
- MLA, used in the humanities
- APA, used in social sciences, education, and business

Anthropology has its own citation style, which is different from any of these. Several sciences have also developed their own distinctive styles:

- CSE for the biological sciences
- AMA for the biomedical sciences, medicine, nursing, and dentistry
- ACS for chemistry
- AIP for physics, plus other styles for astrophysics and astronomy
- AMS for mathematics and computer sciences
- IEEE and ASCE for engineering

I will cover each one, providing clear directions and plenty of examples so you won't have any trouble writing correct citations. That way, you can concentrate on your paper, not on the type of citation you're using. I'll cover each style separately so you can turn directly to the one you need. Using this information, you'll be able to cite books, articles, websites, films, musical performances, government documents—whatever you use in your papers.

Why would you ever want to use different citation styles? Why can't you just pick one and stick with it? Because different fields won't let you. They have designed citation styles to meet their special needs, whether it's genetics or German, and you'll just have to use them. In some sciences, for instance, proper citations list only the author, journal, and pages. They omit the article's title. If you did that in the humanities or social sciences, you'd be incorrect because proper citations for those fields *require* the title. Go figure.

Compare these bibliographic citations for an article of mine:

Chicago	Lipson. Charles. "Why Are Some International Agreements Informal?" *International Organization* 45 (Autumn 1991): 495–538.
APA	Lipson, C. (1991). Why are some international agreements informal? *International Organization, 45,* 495–538.
ACS	Lipson, C. *Int. Org.* **1991,** *45,* 495.

None of these is complicated, but they *are* different. When you leave the chemistry lab to take a course on Shakespeare, you'll leave behind your citation style as well as your beakers. Not to worry. For chemistry papers, just turn to chapter 9. For Shakespeare, turn to chapter 4, which covers MLA citations for the humanities. Both chapters include lots of examples, presented in simple tables, so it won't be "double, double toil and trouble."

Despite their differences, *all these citation styles have the same basic goals*:

- to identify and credit the sources you use; and
- to give readers specific information so they can access these sources themselves, if they wish.

Fortunately, the different styles include a lot of the same information. That means you can write down the same things as you take notes, without worrying about what kind of citations you will ultimately use. You should write down that information as soon as you start taking notes on a new book or article. If you print out or photocopy an article, write all the reference information on the first page. If you do it immediately, you won't forget. You'll need it later for citations. (If you're downloading some of your citations from the web, make sure the information you're getting for each source is accurate *and* complete.)

How these citations will ultimately look depends on which style you use. Chicago notes are either complete citations or shortened versions plus a complete description in the bibliography or in a previous note. Their name comes from their original source, *The Chicago Manual of Style,* published by the University of Chicago Press. This format is sometimes called "Turabian" after a popular book based on that style, Kate Turabian's *A Manual for Writers of Research Papers, Theses, and Dissertations.*[1]

---

1. Kate Turabian, *A Manual for Writers of Research Papers Theses, and Dissertations,* 7th ed., revised by Wayne C. Booth, Gregory C. Colomb, Joseph M. Williams, and the University of Chicago Press Editorial Staff (Chicago: University of Chicago

If you use complete-citation notes, you might not need a bibliography at all since the first note for each item includes all the necessary data. If you use the shortened form, though, you definitely need a bibliography since the notes skip vital information.

Whether you use complete-citation notes or the shortened version, you can place them either at the bottom of each page or at the end of the document. Footnotes and endnotes are identical, except for their placement. Footnotes appear on the same page as the citation in the text. Endnotes are bunched together at the end of the paper, article, chapter, or book. Word processors give you an easy choice between the two.

MLA, APA, and the science citation styles were developed to provide alternative ways of referencing materials. They use in-text citations such as (Stewart 154) or (Stewart, 2004) with full information provided only in a reference list at the end.[2] Because these in-text citations are brief, they require a full bibliography. I'll describe each style in detail and provide lots of examples, just as I will for Chicago citations.

In case you are wondering about the initials: APA stands for the American Psychological Association, which uses this style in its professional journals. MLA stands for the Modern Language Association. Both styles have been adopted well beyond their original fields. APA is widely used in the social sciences, MLA in the humanities. Chicago citations are widely used in both. I will discuss the science styles (and what their initials mean) a little later.

Your department, school, or publisher may prefer one style or even require it, or they might leave it up to you. Check on that as soon as you begin writing papers with citations. Why not do it consistently from the beginning?

Tip on selecting a citation style: Check with your teachers in each class to find out what style citations they prefer. Then use that style consistently.

Press, 2007); *The Chicago Manual of Style,* 16th ed. (Chicago: University of Chicago Press, 2010).

2. Reference lists are similar to bibliographies, but there are some technical differences. In later chapters, I'll explain the details (and nomenclature) for each style. To avoid a needless proliferation of citation styles, I include only the most common ones in each academic field.

Speaking of consistency . . . it's important for proper footnoting. Stick with the same abbreviations and capitalizations, and don't mix styles within a paper. It's easy to write "Volume" in one footnote, "Vol." in another, and "vol." in a third. We all do it, and then we have to correct it. We all abbreviate "chapter" as both "chap." and "ch." Just try your best the first time around and then go back and fix the mistakes when you revise. That's why they invented the search-and-replace function.

My goal here is to provide a one-stop reference so that you can handle nearly all citation issues you'll face, regardless of which style you use and what kinds of items you cite. For each style, I'll show you how to cite books, articles, unpublished papers, websites, and lots more. For specialized documents, such as musical scores or scientific preprints, I show citations only in the fields that actually use them. Physicists often cite preprints, but they don't cite Beethoven. The physics chapter reflects those needs. Students in the humanities not only cite Beethoven; they cite dance performances, plays, and poems. I have included MLA citations for all of them. In case you need to cite something well off the beaten path, I'll explain where to find additional information for each style.

HANGING INDENTS

One final point about shared bibliographic style. Most bibliographies—Chicago, MLA, APA, and some of the sciences—use a special style known as "hanging indents." This applies only to the bibliography and not to footnotes or endnotes. It is the opposite of regular paragraph indention, where the first line is indented and the rest are regular length. In a hanging indent, the first line of each citation is regular length and the rest are indented. For example:

Rothenberg, Gunther E. "Maurice of Nassau, Gustavus Adolphus, Raimondo Montecuccoli, and the 'Military Revolution' of the Seventeenth Century." In *Makers of Modern Strategy from Machiavelli to the Nuclear Age,* edited by Peter Paret, 32–63. Princeton, NJ: Princeton University Press, 1986.
Spooner, Frank C. *Risks at Sea: Amsterdam Insurance and Maritime Europe, 1766–1780.* Cambridge: Cambridge University Press, 1983.

There's a good reason for this unusual format. Hanging indents are designed to make it easy to skim down the list of references and see the authors' names. To remind you to use this format, I'll use it myself when I illustrate references in the citation styles that use it. (The only ones that don't use hanging indents are science styles with numbered citations. It's actually not complicated, and I'll explain it later.)

To make the authors' names stand out further, most bibliographies list their last names first. If an author's name is repeated, however, the styles differ. APA repeats the full name for each citation. MLA uses three hyphens, followed by a period. Chicago uses three em dashes (that is, long dashes), followed by a period.[3]

> Lipson, Beauregard C. H. *Barbecue, Cole Slaw, and Extra Hot Sauce.* Midnight, MS: Hushpuppy, 2011.
> ———. *Mmmmmm! More Gumbo, Please, Ma'am.* Thibodaux, LA: Andouille Press, 2010.

You can arrange hanging indents easily on your word processor. Go to the format feature and, within it, the section on paragraphs. Choose hanging indentation instead of regular or none.

WHERE TO FIND MORE

So far, we have covered some basic issues that apply to most citation styles. There are, of course, lots more questions, some that apply to all styles and some that apply only to one or two. Rather than cover these questions now, I'll handle them in the chapters on individual citation styles and in a final chapter on frequently asked questions (FAQs).

If you have questions that aren't covered in the chapter on your citation style, be sure to check the FAQs chapter. If you still have questions, you can always go to the reference books for each style. Most styles have them (but not all). I'll list them in the chapters for individual styles.

ON TO THE NUTS AND BOLTS

I have organized the references so they are most convenient for you, putting all the documentation for each style in its own chapter.

---

3. Because em dashes are longer than hyphens, they show up differently on-screen and in print. The em dashes show up as a solid line, the hyphens as separate dashes. Three em dashes: ———. Three hyphens: ---. Frankly, you don't need to worry about this for your papers. Use the preferred one if you can, but either is fine.

Chapter 3: Chicago (or Turabian) citations
Chapter 4: MLA citations for the humanities
Chapter 5: APA citations for the social sciences, education, and business
Chapter 6: AAA citations for anthropology and ethnography
Chapter 7: CSE citations for the biological sciences
Chapter 8: AMA citations for the biomedical sciences, medicine, nursing, and dentistry
Chapter 9: ACS citations for chemistry
Chapter 10: Physics, astrophysics, and astronomy citations
Chapter 11: Mathematics, computer science, and engineering citations

Fortunately, they're very straightforward. They're mostly examples, showing you how to cite specific kinds of sources, such as the third edition of a popular book or a chapter in an edited volume. I've included lots of examples of electronic documents, too, from blogs and databases to electronic versions of print documents.

Some of the official style guides do not yet cover the latest forms of electronic communications, such as video blogs or social networking sites. The problem is that you might wish to cite such sources—or perhaps music videos, podcasts, or debates among bloggers—in a paper using one of these styles. My response is to include these newer electronic communications and to base the citations on each style's general rules and citations for similar items. I hope these "unofficial" citations will prove useful.

Don't bother trying to memorize any of these styles. There are simply too many minor details. Just follow the tables, and you'll be able to handle different sources—from journal articles to web pages—in whichever style you need to use. Later, as you write more papers, you'll become familiar with the style you use most.

After explaining each style and answering questions about it, I will also answer some common questions that apply to every style. That's in chapter 12. Now, let's see how to do citations and bibliographies in the specific style you want to use.

Citations in Every Format:
A Quick Guide

3 CHICAGO (OR TURABIAN) CITATIONS

Chicago citations are based on the authoritative *Chicago Manual of Style*. The manual, now in its sixteenth edition, is the bible for references and academic style. A more brief version, covering most aspects of student papers, is Kate Turabian's *A Manual for Writers of Research Papers, Theses, and Dissertations*. This section, however, should cover all you need to document your sources, even if they're unusual.

FULL NOTES, SHORT NOTES, AND BIBLIOGRAPHY

Chicago-style notes come in two flavors, and I include both in this section.[1]

1. A complete first note + short follow-up notes.
   The first note for any item is a full one, giving complete information about the book, article, or other document. Subsequent entries for that item are brief. There is no need for a bibliography since all the information is covered in the first note.
2. Short notes only + bibliography.
   All notes are brief. Full information about the sources appears only in the bibliography.

This means there are three ways to cite individual items. All of them are illustrated in this chapter.

A. Full first notes
B. Short notes
C. Bibliographic entries

---

1. *The Chicago Manual of Style* and Turabian also describe another style, the author-date system. These citations appear in parentheses in the text, listing the author and the date of publication. For example: (Larmore 2011). Full citations appear in a reference list at the end. For simplicity, I have omitted this style since it is similar to APA, discussed in chapter 5.

The first flavor combines A + B, the second combines B + C.

This chapter covers everything from edited books to reference works, from sheet music to online databases, and lots of things in between. To make it easy to find what you need, I've listed them here alphabetically, together with the pages they are on. At the end of this chapter, I answer some questions about using this style.

INDEX OF CHICAGO CITATIONS IN THIS CHAPTER

CHICAGO MANUAL OF STYLE: NOTES AND BIBLIOGRAPHY

Book, one author	Full first note	[99] Charles Lipson, *Reliable Partners: How Democracies Have Made a Separate Peace* (Princeton, NJ: Princeton University Press, 2003), 22–23.

- ▸ This is note number 99 and refers to pages 22–23.
- ▸ Footnotes and endnotes do not have hanging indents. Only the bibliography does.

[99] Pauline W. Chen, *Final Exam: A Surgeon's Reflections on Mortality* (New York: Random House, 2007), 203–6.

- ▸ Chicago (and MLA) abbreviates consecutive page numbers as follows: if the first number is two digits or less, repeat all digits (1–12, 44–68); if the first number is three digits or more and not a multiple of one hundred, include only the changed part (203–6, 345–52, 349–402 *but* 200–23). If this sounds confusing, it is. Fortunately, it's always acceptable to repeat all digits.

Short note   [99] Lipson, *Reliable Partners*, 22–23.
[99] Chen, *Final Exam*, 203–6.

- ▸ Shorten titles to four words or fewer, if possible.

Bibliography   Lipson, Charles. *Reliable Partners: How Democracies Have Made a Separate Peace.* Princeton, NJ: Princeton University Press, 2003.

Chen, Pauline W. *Final Exam: A Surgeon's Reflections on Mortality.* New York: Random House, 2007.

Books, several by same author	First note	[99] William R. Easterly, *The White Man's Burden: Why the West's Efforts to Aid the Rest Have Done So Much Ill and So Little Good* (New York: Penguin, 2006).
[100] William R. Easterly, *The Elusive Quest for Growth: Economists' Adventures and Misadventures in the Tropics* (Cambridge, MA: MIT Press, 2001).

Short note   [99] Easterly, *White Man's Burden.*
                      [100] Easterly, *Elusive Quest for Growth.*

Bibliography   Easterly, William R. *The Elusive Quest for
                      Growth: Economists' Adventures and
                      Misadventures in the Tropics.* Cambridge,
                      MA: MIT Press, 2001.
                      ———. *The White Man's Burden: Why the West's
                      Efforts to Aid the Rest Have Done So Much
                      Ill and So Little Good.* New York: Penguin,
                      2006.
                      ► The repetition of the author's name uses three
                      em dashes (which are simply long dashes),
                      followed by a period. You can find em dashes
                      by digging around in Microsoft Word. Go
                      to "Insert," then "Symbols," then "Special
                      Characters." After you do it once, you can
                      simply copy and paste it. If, for some reason,
                      you can't find the em dash, just use three
                      hyphens.
                      ► List works for each author alphabetically, by
                      title. In alphabetizing, skip any initial article:
                      a, an, the.

Book,   First note   [99] Carol Padden and Tom Humphries, *Inside
multiple   Deaf Culture* (Cambridge, MA: Harvard
authors   University Press, 2005), 61–69.
                                            ► For four or more authors, only use the first
                                            author's name plus "et al." (Latin *et alii,* "and
                                            others"). For example, Carol Padden et al.,
                                            Electing . . .

                      Short note   [99] Padden and Humphries, *Inside Deaf Culture,*
                                            61–69.
                                            ► Titles with four words or fewer are not
                                            shortened.

                      Bibliography   Padden, Carol, and Tom Humphries. *Inside Deaf
                                            Culture.* Cambridge, MA: Harvard University
                                            Press, 2005.
                                            ► Only the first author's name is inverted.
                                            ► List up to ten coauthors in the bibliography. If
                                            there are more, list the first seven, followed by
                                            "et al."

Book, multiple editions	First note	[99] Stuart O. Schweitzer, *Pharmaceutical Economics and Policy*, 2nd ed. (New York: Oxford University Press, 2007). [99] William Strunk Jr. and E. B. White, *The Elements of Style*, 50th anniversary ed. (New York: Longman, 2009), 12.
	Short note	[99] Schweitzer, *Pharmaceutical Economics.* [99] Strunk and White, *Elements of Style*, 12. ▶ To keep the note short, the title doesn't include the initial article (*The Elements of Style*) or the edition number.
	Bibliography	Schweitzer, Stuart O. *Pharmaceutical Economics and Policy.* 2nd ed. New York: Oxford University Press, 2007. Strunk, William, Jr., and E. B. White. *The Elements of Style.* 50th anniversary ed. New York: Longman, 2009.
Book, edited	First note	[99] Karen Bakker, ed., *Eau Canada: The Future of Canada's Water* (Vancouver, BC: University of British Columbia Press, 2007). [99] John Bowker, ed., *Cambridge Illustrated History of Religions* (Cambridge: Cambridge University Press, 2002). [99] David Taras, Maria Bakardjieva, and Frits Pannekoek, eds., *How Canadians Communicate II: Media, Globalization, and Identity* (Calgary, AB: University of Calgary Press, 2007). ▶ Use standard two-letter abbreviations for Canadian provinces.
	Short note	[99] Bakker, *Eau Canada.* ▶ Do not include the abbreviation for editor in short notes. [99] Bowker, *History of Religions.* ▶ Choose the most relevant words when shortening the title. [99] Taras, Bakardjieva, and Pannekoek, *How Canadians Communicate II.*
	Bibliography	Bakker, Karen, ed. *Eau Canada: The Future of Canada's Water.* Vancouver, BC: University of British Columbia Press, 2007.

Bowker, John, ed. *Cambridge Illustrated History of Religions*. Cambridge: Cambridge University Press, 2002.

Taras, David, Maria Bakardjieva, and Frits Pannekoek, eds. *How Canadians Communicate II: Media, Globalization, and Identity*. Calgary, AB: University of Calgary Press, 2007.

Book, anonymous or no author	First note	[99] Anonymous, *Through Our Enemies' Eyes: Osama Bin Laden, Radical Islam, and the Future of America* (Washington, DC: Brassey's, 2003). [99] *Golden Verses of the Pythagoreans* (Whitefish, MT: Kessinger, 2003).
	Short note	[99] Anonymous, *Through Our Enemies' Eyes.* [99] *Golden Verses of Pythagoreans.*
	Bibliography	Anonymous, *Through Our Enemies' Eyes: Osama Bin Laden, Radical Islam, and the Future of America*. Washington, DC: Brassey's, 2003. *Golden Verses of the Pythagoreans*. Whitefish, MT: Kessinger, 2003. ▸ If a book lists "anonymous" as the author, then that word should be included. If no author is listed, then you may list "anonymous" or simply begin with the title.

Book, online and e-books	First note	[99] Charles Dickens, *Great Expectations* (1860–61; Project Gutenberg, 1998), etext 1400, last modified December 1, 2005, http://www.gutenberg.net/etext98/grexp10.txt. ▸ The etext number is helpful but not essential. ▸ If a last-modified or last-updated date is posted, use that; otherwise, include an access date (e.g., "accessed May 5, 2010"). [99] Susan Butler, *East to the Dawn: The Life of Amelia Earhart* (New York: Da Capo, 2009), Kindle edition. ▸ For e-books, include the specific format, such as Kindle or Mobipocket.

	Short note	[99] Dickens, *Great Expectations*.
		[99] Butler, *East to the Dawn*.
	Bibliography	Dickens, Charles. *Great Expectations*. 1860–61. Project Gutenberg, 1998. Etext 1400. Last modified December 1, 2005. http://www.gutenberg.net/etext98/grexp10.txt.
		Butler, Susan. *East to the Dawn: The Life of Amelia Earhart*. New York: Da Capo, 2009. Kindle edition.

Multivolume work	First note	[99] Otto Pflanze, *Bismarck and the Development of Germany*, 3 vols. (Princeton, NJ: Princeton University Press, 1963–90), 1:153.
		[99] Bruce E. Johansen, *Global Warming in the 21st Century*, 3 vols. (Westport, CT: Praeger, 2006), 2:75.
	Short note	[99] Pflanze, *Bismarck*, 1:153.
		[99] Johansen, *Global Warming*, 2:75.
	Bibliography	Pflanze, Otto. *Bismarck and the Development of Germany*. 3 vols. Princeton, NJ: Princeton University Press, 1963–90.
		Johansen, Bruce E. *Global Warming in the 21st Century*. 3 vols. Westport, CT: Praeger, 2006.

Single volume in a multivolume work	First note	[99] Robert A. Caro, *The Years of Lyndon Johnson*, vol. 3, *Master of the Senate* (New York: Knopf, 2002), 237.
		[99] Bruce E. Johansen, *Global Warming in the 21st Century*, vol. 2, *Melting Ice and Warming Seas* (Westport, CT: Praeger, 2006), 71.
		[99] Akira Iriye, *The Globalizing of America*, Cambridge History of American Foreign Relations, edited by Warren I. Cohen, vol. 3 (Cambridge: Cambridge University Press, 1993), 124.
		▸ Caro wrote all three volumes. Iriye wrote only the third volume in a series edited by Cohen.
	Short note	[99] Caro, *Years of Lyndon Johnson*, 3:237.

▶ Or
[99] Caro, *Master of the Senate*, 237.
[99] Johansen, *Global Warming*, 2:71.
▶ Or
[99] Johansen, *Melting Ice and Warming Seas*, 71.
[99] Iriye, *Globalizing of America*, 124.

Bibliography	Caro, Robert A. *The Years of Lyndon Johnson.* Vol. 3, *Master of the Senate.* New York: Knopf, 2002.
	Johansen, Bruce E. *Global Warming in the 21st Century.* Vol. 2, *Melting Ice and Warming Seas.* Westport, CT: Praeger, 2006.
	Iriye, Akira. *The Globalizing of America.* Cambridge History of American Foreign Relations, edited by Warren I. Cohen, vol. 3. Cambridge: Cambridge University Press, 1993.

Reprint of earlier edition	First note	[99] Jacques Barzun, *Simple and Direct: A Rhetoric for Writers*, rev. ed. (1985; repr., Chicago: University of Chicago Press, 1994), 27.
		[99] Adam Smith, *An Inquiry into the Nature and Causes of the Wealth of Nations* (1776), ed. Edwin Cannan (Chicago: University of Chicago Press, 1976).
		▶ The year 1776 appears immediately after the title because that's when Smith's original work appeared. The editor, Edwin Cannan, worked only on its modern publication. The Barzun volume, by contrast, is simply a reprint so the original year appears as part of the publication information.
	Short note	[99] Barzun, *Simple and Direct*, 27.
		[99] Smith, *Wealth of Nations*, vol. I, bk. IV, chap. II: 477.
		▶ This modern edition of Smith is actually a single volume, but it retains the volume numbering of the 1776 original. You could simply cite the page number, but the full citation helps readers with other editions.

	Bibliography	Barzun, Jacques. *Simple and Direct: A Rhetoric for Writers*. 1985. Reprint, Chicago: University of Chicago Press, 1994. Smith, Adam. *An Inquiry into the Nature and Causes of the Wealth of Nations*. 1776. Edited by Edwin Cannan. Chicago: University of Chicago Press, 1976.
Translated volume	First note	[99] Max Weber, *The Protestant Ethic and the Spirit of Capitalism* (1904–5), trans. Talcott Parsons (New York: Charles Scribner's Sons, 1958), 176–77. [99] Alexis de Tocqueville, *Democracy in America* (1835), ed. J. P. Mayer, trans. George Lawrence (New York: HarperCollins, 2000). ▸ Translator and editor are listed in the order they appear on the book's title page. [99] Seamus Heaney, trans., *Beowulf: A New Verse Translation* (New York: Farrar, Straus and Giroux, 2000). ▸ For *Beowulf*, the translator's name appears before the book title because Heaney's is the only name on the title page. (The poem is anonymous.) The same treatment would be given to an editor or compiler whose name appeared alone on the title page.
	Short note	[99] Weber, *Protestant Ethic*, 176–77. [99] Tocqueville, *Democracy in America*. [99] *Beowulf*. ▸ Or [99] Heaney, *Beowulf*.
	Bibliography	Weber, Max. *The Protestant Ethic and the Spirit of Capitalism*. 1904–5. Translated by Talcott Parsons. New York: Charles Scribner's Sons, 1958. Tocqueville, Alexis de. *Democracy in America*. 1835. Edited by J. P. Mayer. Translated by George Lawrence. New York: HarperCollins, 2000. Heaney, Seamus, trans. *Beowulf: A New Verse Translation*. New York: Farrar, Straus and Giroux, 2000.

Chapter in edited book	First note	[99] Benjamin J. Cohen, "The Macrofoundations of Monetary Power," in *International Monetary Power*, ed. David M. Andrews (Ithaca, NY: Cornell University Press, 2006), 31–50.
	Short note	[99] Cohen, "The Macrofoundations of Monetary Power," 31–50.
	Bibliography	Cohen, Benjamin J. "The Macrofoundations of Monetary Power." In *International Monetary Power*, edited by David M. Andrews, 31–50. Ithaca, NY: Cornell University Press, 2006.
Journal article, one author	First note	[99] Adam Meirowitz, "Communication and Bargaining in the Spatial Model," *International Journal of Game Theory* 35 (January 2007): 252.
	Short note	[99] Meirowitz, "Communication and Bargaining," 252. ▸ In a note, refer only to the page(s) cited, if any; in a bibliography, give the page range for the whole article.
	Bibliography	Meirowitz, Adam. "Communication and Bargaining in the Spatial Model." *International Journal of Game Theory* 35 (January 2007): 251–66.
Journal article, multiple authors	First note	[99] William G. Thomas III and Edward L. Ayers, "An Overview: The Differences Slavery Made; A Close Analysis of Two American Communities," *American Historical Review* 108 (December 2003): 1301–2. [99] Jeffery J. Mondak et al., "Does Familiarity Breed Contempt? The Impact of Information on Mass Attitudes toward Congress," *American Journal of Political Science* 51 (January 2007): 46. ▸ For four or more authors, only use the first author's name plus "et al."
	Short note	[99] Thomas and Ayers, "Differences Slavery Made," 1301–2.

[99] Mondak et al., "Does Familiarity Breed Contempt?," 46.

Bibliography   Thomas, William G., III, and Edward L. Ayers. "An Overview: The Differences Slavery Made; a Close Analysis of Two American Communities." *American Historical Review* 108 (December 2003): 1299–307.

Mondak, Jeffery J., Edward G. Carmines, Robert Huckfeldt, Dona-Gene Mitchell, and Scot Schraufnagel. "Does Familiarity Breed Contempt? The Impact of Information on Mass Attitudes toward Congress." *American Journal of Political Science* 51 (January 2007): 34–48.

▸ Only the first author's name is inverted.

▸ List up to ten coauthors in the bibliography. If there are more, list the first seven, followed by "et al."

Journal article, online

First note   [99] Janice B. Stockigt and Michael Talbot, "Two More New Vivaldi Finds in Dresden," *Eighteenth-Century Music* 3, no. 1 (Spring 2006): 37, accessed May 5, 2010, doi:10.1017/S1478570606000480.

▸ The string of numbers at the end of the citation (except for the final period) is called a Digital Object Identifier (DOI). A DOI—a permanent ID—is preferable to a URL. (Pasting the DOI into a DOI resolver, available from CrossRef .org, will direct you to the article—wherever it is posted.) If you don't see a DOI, list the URL (usually, the address in your browser's location bar) instead.

Short note   [99] Stockigt and Talbot, "Two More New Vivaldi Finds," 37.

Bibliography   Stockigt, Janice B., and Michael Talbot. "Two More New Vivaldi Finds in Dresden." *Eighteenth-Century Music* 3, no. 1 (Spring 2006): 35–61. Accessed May 5, 2010. doi:10.1017/S1478570606000480.

Journal article, foreign language	First note	[99] Zvi Uri Ma'oz, "Y a-t-il des juifs sans synagogue?," *Revue des Études Juives* 163 (juillet–décembre 2004): 485. ▸ Or [99] Zvi Uri Ma'oz, "Y a-t-il des juifs sans synagogue?" [Are there Jews without a synagogue?], *Revue des Études Juives* 163 (juillet–décembre 2004): 485.
	Short note	[99] Ma'oz, "Y a-t-il des juifs sans synagogue?," 485.
	Bibliography	Ma'oz, Zvi Uri. "Y a-t-il des juifs sans synagogue?" *Revue des Études Juives* 163 (juillet–décembre 2004): 483–93. ▸ Or Ma'oz, Zvi Uri. "Y a-t-il des juifs sans synagogue?" [Are there Jews without a synagogue?]. *Revue des Études Juives* 163 (juillet–décembre 2004): 483–93.
Newspaper or magazine article, no author	First note	[99] "State Senator's Indictment Details Demands on Staff," *New York Times*, February 11, 2007, national edition, 23. ▸ This refers to page 23. You may omit page numbers, if you wish, since many newspapers have different editions with different pagination.
	Short note	[99] "State Senator's Indictment," *New York Times*, 23. ▸ Since newspapers are usually omitted from the bibliography, use a full citation for the first reference.
	Bibliography	▸ Newspaper articles are left out of bibliographies, but you can include an especially important article: "State Senator's Indictment Details Demands on Staff." *New York Times*, February 11, 2007, national edition, 23.
Newspaper or magazine article, with author	First note	[99] David M. Halbfinger, "Politicians Are Doing Hollywood Star Turns," *New York Times*, February 6, 2007, national edition, B1, B7.

► You may omit pagination from newspapers, if you wish, since these vary from edition to edition.

[99] Paul Theroux, "Michael Jackson's Neverland: 'Has Anyone Seen My Childhood?,'" *Architectural Digest*, November 2009, 103.

► Articles in magazines intended for general audiences are treated the same as newspaper articles and cited by date only. Some magazines are more like journals. If you are unsure what you're citing—journal or magazine—look for a volume number. If you spot one without too much trouble, cite as a journal.

Short note

[99] Halbfinger, "Politicians Are Doing Hollywood," B1, B7.
[99] Theroux, "Michael Jackson's Neverland," 103.

Bibliography

► Newspaper and magazine articles are rarely included in bibliographies, but you can include an especially important article:

Halbfinger, David M. "Politicians Are Doing Hollywood Star Turns." *New York Times*, February 6, 2007, national edition, B1, B7.

Newspaper or magazine article, online

First note

[99] Charles Babington, "Democrats Urge Tighter FCC Rules," *Washington Post*, February 2, 2007, accessed May 5, 2010, http://www.washingtonpost.com/wp-dyn/content/article/2007/02/01/AR2007020101997.html.

Short note

[99] Babington, "Democrats Urge Tighter FCC Rules."

Bibliography

► Rarely included, but you may include an especially important article:

Babington, Charles. "Democrats Urge Tighter FCC Rules." *Washington Post,* February 5, 2007. Accessed May 5, 2010. http://www.washingtonpost.com/wp-dyn/content/article/2007/02/01/AR2007020101997.html.

Review	First note	[99] Joseph H. Lane, review of *A Kinder, Gentler America: Melancholia and the Mythical 1950s*, by Mary Caputi, *Perspectives on Politics* 4 (December 2006): 749–50. [99] Niall Ferguson, "Ameliorate, Contain, Coerce, Destroy," review of *The Utility of Force: The Art of War in the Modern World*, by Rupert Smith, *New York Times Book Review*, February 4, 2007, 14–15.
	Short note	[99] Lane, review of *Kinder, Gentler America*. [99] Ferguson, "Ameliorate, Contain, Coerce, Destroy." ▸ Or [99] Ferguson, review of *The Utility of Force*.
	Bibliography	Lane, Joseph H. Review of *A Kinder, Gentler America: Melancholia and the Mythical 1950s*, by Mary Caputi. *Perspectives on Politics* 4 (December 2006): 749–50. Ferguson, Niall. "Ameliorate, Contain, Coerce, Destroy." Review of *The Utility of Force: The Art of War in the Modern World*, by Rupert Smith. *New York Times Book Review*, February 4, 2007, 14–15.
Unpublished paper, thesis, or dissertation	First note	[99] Ashley Leeds, "Interests, Institutions, and Foreign Policy Consistency" (paper presented at the Program on International Politics, Economics, and Security, University of Chicago, February 15, 2007), 1–25. [99] Lance Noble, "One Goal, Multiple Strategies: Engagement in Sino-American WTO Accession Negotiations" (master's thesis, University of British Columbia, 2006), 15. [99] Mihwa Choi, "Contesting Imaginaires in Death Rituals during the Northern Song Dynasty" (PhD diss., University of Chicago, 2008), ProQuest (AAT 3300426). ▸ If you consult a paper through a commercial database, include the name of the database and a document ID.

Short note   [99] Leeds, "Interests, Institutions, and Foreign Policy."
[99] Noble, "One Goal, Multiple Strategies."
[99] Choi, "Contesting Imaginaires."

Bibliography   Leeds, Ashley. "Interests, Institutions, and Foreign Policy Consistency." Paper presented at the Program on International Politics, Economics, and Security, University of Chicago, February 15, 2007.

Noble, Lance. "One Goal, Multiple Strategies: Engagement in Sino-American WTO Accession Negotiations." Master's thesis, University of British Columbia, 2006.

Choi, Mihwa. "Contesting Imaginaires in Death Rituals during the Northern Song Dynasty." PhD diss., University of Chicago, 2008. ProQuest (AAT 3300426).

Preprint or working paper

First note   [99] John C. Rodda et al., "A Comparative Study of the Magnitude, Frequency and Distribution of Intense Rainfall in the United Kingdom," preprint, October 9, 2009, accessed May 5, 2010, http://precedings.nature.com/documents/3847/version/1.
[99] Catharine P. Wells, "Langdell and the Invention of Legal Doctrine," University of Southern California Legal Studies Working Paper Series, working paper 51, September 2009, accessed May 5, 2010. http://law.bepress.com/usclwps/lss/art51.

Short note   [99] Rodda et al., "Rainfall in the United Kingdom."
[99] Wells, "Langdell."

Bibliography   Rodda, John C., Max A. Little, Harvey J. E. Rodda, and Patrick E. McSharry. "A Comparative Study of the Magnitude, Frequency and Distribution of Intense Rainfall in the United Kingdom." Preprint, October 9, 2009. Accessed May 5, 2010. http://precedings.nature.com/documents/3847/version/1.

Wells, Catharine P. "Langdell and the Invention of Legal Doctrine." University of Southern California Legal Studies Working Paper Series, working paper 51, September 2009. Accessed May 5, 2010. http://law.bepress.com/usclwps/lss/art51.

Abstract	First note	[99] Carlos Barahona and Sarah Levy, "The Best of Both Worlds: Producing National Statistics Using Participatory Methods," abstract, *World Development* 35 (February 2007): 326–41, accessed May 5, 2010, doi:10.1016/j.worlddev.2006.10.006. [99] John Hatchard, "Combating Transnational Crime in Africa: Problems and Perspectives," *Journal of African Law* 50 (October 2006): 145–60, abstract in *African Studies Abstracts Online* 17, abstract no. 21 (2007): 28, accessed May 5, 2010, http://hdl.handle.net/1887/11948. ▸ For abstracts consulted online, include a DOI or URL. If the source recommends a URL that's different from the one in your browser's address bar, use theirs (the URL in the Hatchard example is a special type similar to a DOI).
	Short note	[99] Barahona and Levy, "Best of Both Worlds," 326–41. [99] Hatchard, "Combating Transnational Crime in Africa," 28.
	Bibliography	Barahona, Carlos, and Sarah Levy. "The Best of Both Worlds: Producing National Statistics Using Participatory Methods." Abstract. *World Development* 35 (February 2007): 326–41. Accessed May 5, 2010. doi:10.1016/j.worlddev.2006.10.006. Hatchard, John. "Combating Transnational Crime in Africa: Problems and Perspectives." *Journal of African Law* 50 (October 2006): 145–60. Abstract in *African Studies Abstracts Online* 17, Abstract No. 21 (2007): 28. Accessed May 5, 2010. http://hdl.handle.net/1887/11948.

Microfilm, microfiche	First note	[99] Martin Luther King Jr., *FBI File*, ed. David J. Garrow (Frederick, MD: University Publications of America, 1984), microform. [99] Alice Irving Abbott, *Circumstantial Evidence* (New York: W. B. Smith, 1882), in *American Fiction, 1774–1910* (Woodbridge, CT: Gale/Primary Source Microfilm, 1998), microfilm, reel A-1.
	Short note	[99] King, *FBI File*, 11:23–24. [99] Abbott, *Circumstantial Evidence*, 73.
	Bibliography	King, Martin Luther, Jr. *FBI File*. Edited by David J. Garrow. Frederick, MD: University Publications of America, 1984. Microform. Abbott, Alice Irving. *Circumstantial Evidence*. New York: W. B. Smith, 1882. In *American Fiction, 1774–1910*. Reel A-1. Woodbridge, CT: Gale/Primary Source Microfilm, 1998. ▸ You can omit any mention of microfilm or microfiche if it simply preserves a source in its original form. Just cite the work as if it were the published version. So, to cite the Abbott book: Abbott, Alice Irving. *Circumstantial Evidence*. New York: W. B. Smith, 1882.
Archival materials and manuscript collections, hard copies and online	First note	[99] Isaac Franklin to R. C. Ballard, February 28, 1831, series 1.1, folder 1, Rice Ballard Papers, Southern Historical Collection, Wilson Library, University of North Carolina, Chapel Hill. ▸ Here is the order of items within the citation: 1. Author and brief description of the item 2. Date, if possible 3. Identification number for item or manuscript 4. Title of the series or collection 5. Library (or depository) and its location; for well-known libraries and archives, the location may be omitted. [99] Mary Swift Lamson, "An Account of the Beginning of the B.Y.W.C.A.," MS, [n.d.], and accompanying letter, 1891, series I, I-A-2,

Boston YWCA Papers, Schlesinger Library, Radcliffe Institute for Advanced Study, Harvard University.

▸ "MS" = manuscript = papers (plural: "MSS")

99 Sigismundo Taraval, Journal recounting Indian uprisings in Baja California [handwritten MS], 1734–1737, ¶ 23, Edward E. Ayer Manuscript Collection no. 1240, Newberry Library, Chicago, IL.

▸ This journal has numbered paragraphs. Page numbers, paragraphs, or other identifiers aid readers.

99 Horatio Nelson Taft, Diary, February 20, 1862, p. 149 (vol. 1, January 1, 1861–April 11, 1862), Manuscript Division, Library of Congress, accessed May 5, 2010, http://memory.loc.gov /ammem/tafthtml/tafthome.html.

99 Henrietta Szold to Rose Jacobs, February 3, 1932, reel 1, book 1, Rose Jacobs–Alice L. Seligsberg Collection, Judaica Microforms, Brandeis Library, Waltham, MA.

▸ Abbreviations: When a collection's name and location are often repeated, they may be abbreviated after the first use:

99 Henrietta Szold to Rose Jacobs, March 9, 1936, A/125/112, Central Zionist Archives, Jerusalem (hereafter cited as CZA).

100 Szold to Eva Stern, July 27, 1936, A/125/912, CZA.

Short note

99 Isaac Franklin to R. C. Ballard, February 28, 1831, series 1.1, folder 1, Rice Ballard Papers.

▸ Short-form citation varies for archival items. The main concerns are readers' convenience and the proximity of full information in nearby notes.

99 Mary Swift Lamson, "Beginning of the B.Y.W.C.A.," MS, [1891], Boston YWCA Papers, Schlesinger Library.

99 Sigismundo Taraval, Journal recounting Indian uprisings in Baja California, Edward E. Ayer Manuscript Collection, Newberry Library.

▸ Or

[99] Taraval, Journal, Ayer MS Collection, Newberry Library.

[99] Horatio Nelson Taft, Diary, February 20, 1862, 149.

[99] Henrietta Szold to Rose Jacobs, February 3, 1932, reel 1, book 1, Rose Jacobs–Alice L. Seligsberg Collection.

[100] Szold to Jacobs, March 9, 1936, A/125/112, CZA.

[101] Szold to Eva Stern, July 27, 1936, A/125/912, CZA.

Bibliography   Rice Ballard Papers. Southern Historical Collection. Wilson Library. University of North Carolina, Chapel Hill.

▸ In footnotes and endnotes, the specific archival item is usually listed first because it is the most important element in the note. For example: Isaac Franklin to R. C. Ballard, February 28, 1831. In bibliographies, however, the collection itself is usually listed first because it is more important. Individual items are not mentioned in the bibliography *unless* only one item is cited from a particular collection.

Boston YWCA Papers. Schlesinger Library. Radcliffe Institute for Advanced Study, Harvard University.

▸ Or

Lamson, Mary Swift. "An Account of the Beginning of the B.Y.W.C.A." MS, [n.d.], and accompanying letter, 1891. Boston YWCA Papers. Schlesinger Library. Radcliffe Institute for Advanced Study, Harvard University.

▸ If Lamson's account is the only item cited from these papers, then it would be listed in the bibliography.

Ayer, Edward E. Manuscript Collection. Newberry Library, Chicago, IL.

Taft, Horatio Nelson. Diary. Vol. 1, January 1, 1861–April 11, 1862. Manuscript Division, Library of Congress. Accessed May 5, 2010. http://memory.loc.gov/ammem/tafthtml /tafthome.html.

Rose Jacobs–Alice L. Seligsberg Collection.
Judaica Microforms. Brandeis Library,
Waltham, MA.
Central Zionist Archives, Jerusalem.

Encyclopedia, hard copy and online	First note	[99] *Encyclopaedia Britannica*, 15th ed., s.vv. "Balkans: History," "World War I."

▶ The abbreviation s.v. (*sub verbo*) means "under the word." Plural: s.vv.

▶ You must include the edition but, according to *The Chicago Manual of Style*, you can omit the publisher, location, and page numbers for well-known references like the *Encyclopaedia Britannica*.

[99] *Encyclopaedia Britannica Online*, s.v. "Balkans," accessed May 5, 2010, http://www.britannica.com/EBchecked/topic/50325/Balkans.

▶ Some encyclopedias post a recommended URL alongside each article; use that one instead of the URL that appears in your browser's address bar.

[99] George Graham, "Behaviorism," in *Stanford Encyclopedia of Philosophy*, article published May 26, 2000, revised July 30, 2007, accessed May 5, 2010, http://plato.stanford.edu/entries/behaviorism/.

▶ Or

[99] *Stanford Encyclopedia of Philosophy*, "Behaviorism," by George Graham, article published May 26, 2000, revised July 30, 2007, accessed May 5, 2010, http://plato.stanford.edu/entries/behaviorism/.

[99] *Wikipedia*, "Stamford Raffles," last modified October 15, 2009, accessed May 5, 2010, http://en.wikipedia.org/wiki/Stamford_Raffles.

▶ If an article lists a publication date, include it; a last-modified date can be used instead. Also include an access date.

Short note

[99] *Encyclopaedia Britannica*, s.v. "World War I."

[99] *Encyclopaedia Britannica Online*, s.v. "Balkans."

[99] Graham, "Behaviorism."

▸ Or

[99] *Stanford Encyclopedia*, "Behaviorism."

[99] *Wikipedia*, "Stamford Raffles."

Bibliography	▸ Well-known encyclopedias are not normally listed in bibliographies, but you may wish to include articles from more specialized encyclopedias, especially if they're authored.

Graham, George. "Behaviorism." In *Stanford Encyclopedia of Philosophy*. Article published May 26, 2000. Revised July 30, 2007. Accessed May 5, 2010. http://plato.stanford.edu/entries/behaviorism/.

▸ Or

Stanford Encyclopedia of Philosophy. "Behaviorism," by George Graham. Article published May 26, 2000. Revised July 30, 2007. Accessed May 5, 2010. http://plato.stanford.edu/entries/behaviorism/.

Reference book, hard copy and online	First note	[99] *Reference Guide to World Literature*, 3rd ed., 2 vols., ed. Sara Pendergast and Tom Pendergast (Detroit: St. James Press, 2003).

[99] *Reference Guide to World Literature*, 3rd ed., ed. Sara Pendergast and Tom Pendergast, Gale Virtual Reference Library (Thomson/Gale, 2003), e-book.

[99] Edmund Cusick, "The Snow Queen, story by Hans Christian Andersen," in *Reference Guide to World Literature*, 3rd ed., 2 vols., ed. Sara Pendergast and Tom Pendergast (Detroit: St. James Press, 2003), 2:1511–12.

[99] "Obama Marks Holocaust in Germany, D-Day in France; Visits WWII Sites in Buchenwald, Normandy," June 11, 2009, *Facts On File World News Digest*, accession no. 2009492010.

Short note	[99] *Reference Guide to World Literature*.

[99] Cusick, "Snow Queen," 2:1511–12.

[99] "Obama Marks Holocaust."

Bibliography		*Reference Guide to World Literature.* 3rd ed. 2 vols., edited by Sara Pendergast and Tom Pendergast. Detroit: St. James Press, 2003.
		Reference Guide to World Literature. 3rd ed., edited by Sara Pendergast and Tom Pendergast. Gale Virtual Reference Library. Thomson/Gale, 2003. E-book.
		Cusick, Edmund. "The Snow Queen, story by Hans Christian Andersen." In *Reference Guide to World Literature.* 3rd ed. 2 vols., edited by Sara Pendergast and Tom Pendergast, 2:1511–12. Detroit: St. James Press, 2003.
		"Obama Marks Holocaust in Germany, D-Day in France; Visits WWII Sites in Buchenwald, Normandy." June 11, 2009. *Facts On File World News Digest.* Accession no. 2009492010.

Dictionary, hard copy, online, and CD-ROM	First note	[99] *Merriam-Webster's Collegiate Dictionary*, 11th ed., s.v. "chronology."
		▸ You must include the edition but can omit the publisher, location, and page numbers for well-known references like *Merriam-Webster's.*
		[99] *Compact Edition of the Oxford English Dictionary*, s.vv. "class, *n.*," "state, *n.*"
		▸ The words "class" and "state" can be either nouns or verbs, and this reference is to the nouns.
		[99] *Dictionary.com Unabridged*, s.v. "status," accessed May 5, 2010, http://dictionary.reference.com/browse/status.
		[99] *American Heritage Dictionary of the English Language*, 4th ed., CD-ROM.
	Short note	[99] *Merriam-Webster's*, s.v. "chronology."
		[99] *Compact O.E.D.*, s.vv. "class, *n.*," "state, *n.*"
		[99] *Dictionary.com*, s.v. "status."
		[99] *American Heritage* on CD-ROM.
	Bibliography	▸ Standard dictionaries are not normally listed in bibliographies, but you may wish to include more specialized reference works:

> *Middle English Dictionary, W.2,* edited by
> Robert E. Lewis. Ann Arbor: University of
> Michigan Press, 1999.
> *Middle English Dictionary.* Ann Arbor: Regents of
> the University of Michigan, 2001. Accessed
> May 5, 2010. http://quod.lib.umich.edu/m
> /med/.

Bible, Koran (Qur'an)	First note	[99] Genesis 1:1, 1:3–5, 2:4.

[99] Genesis 1:1, 1:3–5, 2:4 (New Revised Standard Version).

► Books of the Bible can be abbreviated: Gen. 1:1.

► Abbreviations for the next four books are Exod., Lev., Num., and Deut. Abbreviations for other books are easily found with a web search for "abbreviations + Bible."

[99] Koran 18:65–82.

Short note

[99] Genesis 1:1, 1:3–5, 2:4.
[99] Koran 18:65–82.

Bibliography

► References to the Bible, Koran, and other sacred texts are not normally included in the bibliography. You may include them, however, if you wish to show that you are using a particular version or translation, such as:

Tanakh: The Holy Scriptures: The New JPS Translation according to the Traditional Hebrew Text. Philadelphia: Jewish Publication Society, 1985.

► Thou shalt omit the Divine Author's name.

Classical works	First note	► Ordinarily, classical Greek and Latin works

are referred to in the text itself or in notes. They are not included in the bibliography except to reference the specific translation or commentary by a modern author. Here is an in-text reference:

In Pericles' Funeral Oration (2.34–46), Thucydides gives us one of history's most moving speeches.

▶ If you do need to include a note, here is the format:

99 Plato, *The Republic*, trans. R. E. Allen (New Haven, CT: Yale University Press, 2006).

99 Virgil, *The Aeneid*, introd. Bernard Knox, trans. Robert Fagles (New York: Viking, 2006).

Short note

99 Plato, *Republic* 3.212b–414b.

99 Virgil, *Aeneid* 5.6–31.

Bibliography

▶ Classical Greek and Latin works are not normally included in the bibliography except to reference the specific translation or commentary by a modern author.

Plato. *The Republic*. Translated by R. E. Allen. New Haven, CT: Yale University Press, 2006.

Virgil. *The Aeneid*. Introduction by Bernard Knox. Translated by Robert Fagles. New York: Viking, 2006.

Speech, academic talk, or course lecture

First note

99 David J. Skorton, "State of the University Speech" (Cornell University, Ithaca, NY, October 27, 2006).

99 Ira Katznelson, "At the Court of Chaos: Political Science in an Age of Perpetual Fear" (presidential address, annual meeting of the American Political Science Association, Philadelphia, PA, August 31, 2006).

99 Gary Sick, lecture on U.S. policy toward Iran (U.S. Foreign Policy Making in the Persian Gulf, course taught at Columbia University, New York, March 22, 2007).

▶ The title of Professor Sick's talk is not capitalized or in quotes because it is a regular course lecture and does not have a specific title. I have given a description, but you could simply call it a lecture and omit the description. For example: Gary Sick, untitled lecture (U.S. Foreign . . .).

Short note

99 Skorton, "State of the University Speech."

▶ Or, to differentiate it from Skorton's addresses in subsequent years:

[99] Skorton, "State of the University Speech," 2006.
[99] Katznelson, "At the Court of Chaos."
[99] Sick, lecture on U.S. policy toward Iran.

Bibliography

Skorton, David J. "State of the University Speech." Cornell University, Ithaca, NY, October 27, 2006.

Katznelson, Ira. "At the Court of Chaos: Political Science in an Age of Perpetual Fear." Presidential address, annual meeting of the American Political Science Association, Philadelphia, PA, August 31, 2006.

Sick, Gary. Lecture on U.S. policy toward Iran. U.S. Foreign Policy Making in the Persian Gulf, course taught at Columbia University, New York, March 22, 2007.

Personal communication or interview

First note

[99] J. M. Coetzee, personal interview, December 8, 2009.
[99] Nicolas Sarkozy, telephone interview (Internet), May 5, 2010.
[99] George Lucas, video interview (Internet/Skype), May 5, 2010.
[99] Anonymous U.S. Marine, recently returned from Afghanistan, interview by author, May 5, 2010.
[99] Discussion with senior official at Department of Homeland Security, Washington, DC, January 7, 2010.

▶ Sometimes you may not wish to reveal the source of an interview or conversation, or you may have promised not to reveal your source. If so, then you should (a) reveal as much descriptive data as you can, such as "a police officer who works with an anti-gang unit," instead of just "a police officer" and (b) explain to readers, in a footnote, why you are omitting names, such as "All interviews with State Department officials were conducted with guarantees of anonymity because the officials were not authorized to disclose this information to the public."

[99] Margaret MacMillan, "On Her New Book, *Nixon in China: The Week That Changed the World*," interview by Kenneth Whyte, *Macleans*, September 27, 2006, accessed May 5, 2010, http://www.macleans.ca/culture/books/article.jsp?content=20061002_133865_133865.

Short note

[99] J. M. Coetzee, personal interview, December 8, 2009.
[99] George Lucas, video interview, May 5, 2010.
[99] Nicolas Sarkozy, telephone interview, May 5, 2010.
[99] Anonymous U.S. Marine, interview by author, May 5, 2010.
[99] Discussion with senior official at Department of Homeland Security, January 7, 2010.
[99] MacMillan, "On *Nixon in China*."

Bibliography

▶ Interviews should be included in the bibliography if they are in print, online, or archived because they are available to other researchers. Personal interviews and communications that are not accessible to others should be described fully in the notes and omitted from the bibliography. Hence, there is a bibliographic item for Macmillan but none for Coetzee, Sarkozy, Lucas, or the anonymous U.S. Marine or senior official.

MacMillan, Margaret. "On Her New Book, *Nixon in China: The Week That Changed the World*." Interview by Kenneth Whyte. *Macleans,* September 27, 2006. Accessed May 5, 2010. http://www.macleans.ca/culture/books/article.jsp?content=20061002_133865_133865.

Poem   First note

[99] Elizabeth Bishop, "The Fish," in *The Complete Poems, 1927–1979* (New York: Noonday Press/Farrar, Straus and Giroux, 1983), 42–44.
[99] Walt Whitman, "Song of Myself," in *Leaves of Grass* (Philadelphia: David McKay, 1891–92), sec. 51, p. 78, accessed May 5, 2010, http://whitmanarchive.org/published/LG/1891/whole.html.

	Short note	[99] Bishop, "The Fish," 42–44.
		[99] Whitman, "Song of Myself," sec. 51, p. 78.
	Bibliography	Bishop, Elizabeth. "The Fish." In *The Complete Poems, 1927–1979*, 42–44. New York: Noonday Press/Farrar, Straus and Giroux, 1983.
		Walt Whitman. "Song of Myself." In *Leaves of Grass*, 29–79. Philadelphia: David McKay, 1891–92. Accessed May 5, 2010. http://whitmanarchive.org/published/LG/1891/whole.html.

Play, text	First note	[99] Shakespeare, *Hamlet, Prince of Denmark*, 2.1.1–9.
		▸ Refers to act 2, scene 1, lines 1–9.
		▸ If you wish to cite a specific edition, then:
		[99] William Shakespeare, *Hamlet, Prince of Denmark*, ed. Constance Jordan (New York: Pearson/Longman, 2005).
		[99] William Shakespeare, *The Three-Text Hamlet: Parallel Texts of the First and Second Quartos and First Folio*, ed. Bernice W. Kliman and Paul Bertram, introd. Eric Rasmussen (New York: AMS Press, 2003).
		[99] William Shakespeare, *Hamlet, Prince of Denmark* (1600–1601; University of Virginia Library, Electronic Text Center, 1998), accessed May 5, 2010, http://etext.virginia.edu/toc/modeng/public/MobHaml.html.
	Short note	[99] Shakespeare, *Hamlet*, 2.1.1–9.
	Bibliography	Shakespeare, William. *Hamlet, Prince of Denmark*. Edited by Constance Jordan. New York: Pearson/Longman, 2005.
		Shakespeare, William. *The Three-Text Hamlet: Parallel Texts of the First and Second Quartos and First Folio*. Edited by Bernice W. Kliman and Paul Bertram. Introduction by Eric Rasmussen. New York: AMS Press, 2003.
		Shakespeare, William. *Hamlet, Prince of Denmark*. 1600–1601. University of

Virginia Library, Electronic Text Center, 1998. Accessed May 5, 2010. http://etext .virginia.edu/toc/modeng/public/MobHaml .html.

Performance of play or dance	First note	[99] *Bitter Suite*, choreography by Jorma Elo, music by Felix Mendelssohn and Claudio Monteverdi, Hubbard Street Dance Chicago, Harris Theater for Music and Dance at Millennium Park, Chicago, October 2, 2009. [99] *Fake*, written and directed by Eric Simonson, performed by Kate Arrington, Francis Guinan, and Alan Wilder, Steppenwolf Theatre, Chicago, October 28, 2009. ▸ If you are concentrating on one person or one position such as director, put that person's name first. For example, if you are concentrating on Kate Arrington's acting: [99] Kate Arrington, performance, *Fake*, written and directed by Eric Simonson, . . .
	Short note	[99] *Bitter Suite*. [99] *Fake*.
	Bibliography	*Bitter Suite*. Choreography by Jorma Elo. Music by Felix Mendelssohn and Claudio Monteverdi. Hubbard Street Dance Chicago. Harris Theater for Music and Dance at Millennium Park, Chicago, October 2, 2009. *Fake*. Written and directed by Eric Simonson. Performed by Kate Arrington, Francis Guinan, and Alan Wilder. Steppenwolf Theatre, Chicago, October 28, 2009. ▸ Or, if you are concentrating on Arrington's acting: Kate Arrington, performance. *Fake*. Written and directed by Eric Simonson, . . .
Television program	First note	[99] *Seinfeld*, "The Soup Nazi," episode 116, November 2, 1995. ▸ Or, a fuller citation: [99] *Seinfeld*, "The Soup Nazi," episode 116, directed by Andy Ackerman, written by Spike

Feresten, performed by Jerry Seinfeld, Jason Alexander, Julia Louis-Dreyfus, Michael Richards, Alexandra Wentworth, and Larry Thomas, NBC, November 2, 1995.

[99] *30 Rock*, "Season 4," season 4, episode 1, directed by Don Scardino, written by Tina Fey, performed by Tina Fey, Tracy Morgan, Jane Krakowski, Jack McBrayer, Scott Adsit, Judah Friedlander, and Alec Baldwin, aired October 15, 2009 (NBC), accessed October 21, 2009, http://www.hulu.com/30-rock.

> ► Yes, this first episode of the fourth season was actually called "Season 4." Episode numbers are helpful. So are original air dates for shows you watched in a medium other than broadcast.

Short note	[99] *Seinfeld*, "Soup Nazi." [99] *30 Rock*, "Season 4."
Bibliography	*Seinfeld*, "The Soup Nazi." Episode 116. Directed by Andy Ackerman. Written by Spike Feresten. Performed by Jerry Seinfeld, Jason Alexander, Julia Louis-Dreyfus, Michael Richards, Alexandra Wentworth, and Larry Thomas. NBC, November 2, 1995. *30 Rock*, "Season 4." Season 4, episode 1. Directed by Don Scardino. Written by Tina Fey. Performed by Tina Fey, Tracy Morgan, Jane Krakowski, Jack McBrayer, Scott Adsit, Judah Friedlander, and Alec Baldwin. Aired October 15, 2009, on NBC. Accessed October 21, 2009. http://www.hulu.com/30-rock.
Film First note	[99] *Godfather II*, DVD, directed by Francis Ford Coppola (1974; Los Angeles: Paramount Home Video, 2003). > ► If you wish to cite individual scenes, which are accessible on DVDs, treat them like chapters in books. "Murder of Fredo," *Godfather II* . . .
Short note	[99] *Godfather II*.

	Bibliography	*Godfather II*, DVD. Directed by Francis Ford Coppola. Performed by Al Pacino, Robert De Niro, Robert Duvall, Diane Keaton. Screenplay by Francis Ford Coppola and Mario Puzo based on novel by Mario Puzo. 1974; Paramount Home Video, 2003.
		▸ Title, director, studio, and year of release are all required. So is the year the video recording was released, if that's what you are citing.
		▸ Optional: the actors, producers, screenwriters, editors, cinematographers, and other information. You can include what you need for your paper, in order of their importance to your analysis. Their names appear between the title and the distributor.
Artwork, original	First note	[99] Jacopo Robusti Tintoretto, *The Birth of John the Baptist*, ca. 1550, Hermitage, St. Petersburg.
		▸ If the exact date of an artwork is not available, give an approximate one. A painting from "circa 1550" would be abbreviated "ca. 1550."
	Short note	[99] Tintoretto, *Birth of John the Baptist*.
	Bibliography	▸ Do not include any artwork, sculptures, or photographs in the bibliography.
Artwork, reproduction	First note	[99] Jacopo Robusti Tintoretto, *The Birth of John the Baptist*, 1550s, in Tom Nichols, *Tintoretto: Tradition and Identity* (London: Reaktion Books, 1999), 47.
	Short note	[99] Tintoretto, *Birth of John the Baptist*.
	Bibliography	▸ Do not include any artwork, sculptures, or photographs in the bibliography.
Artwork, online	First note	[99] Jacopo Robusti Tintoretto, *The Birth of John the Baptist*, 1550s, Hermitage, St. Petersburg, accessed May 5, 2010, http://www.hermitagemuseum.org/.
		[99] Jacopo Robusti Tintoretto, *The Birth of John the Baptist* (detail), 1550s, Hermitage, St. Petersburg, accessed May 5, 2010, http://cgfa.acropolisinc.com/t/p-tintore1.htm.

	Short note	[99] Tintoretto, *Birth of John the Baptist.*
	Bibliography	▸ Do not include any artwork, sculptures, or photographs in the bibliography.
Photograph	First note	[99] Ansel Adams, *Monolith, the Face of Half Dome, Yosemite National Park*, 1927, Art Institute, Chicago.
	Short note	[99] Adams, *Monolith.*
	Bibliography	▸ Do not include any artwork, sculptures, or photographs in the bibliography.
Photograph, online	First note	[99] Ansel Adams, *Monolith, the Face of Half Dome, Yosemite National Park*, 1927, Art Institute, Chicago, accessed May 5, 2010, http://www.hctc.commnet.edu/artmuseum /anseladams/details/pdf/monlith.pdf.
	Short note	[99] Adams, *Monolith.*
	Bibliography	▸ Do not include any artwork, sculptures, or photographs in the bibliography.
Figures: map, chart, graph, or table	Credit for figure or table	▸ Citation for a map, chart, graph, or table normally appears as a credit below the item rather than as a footnote or endnote. *Source*: Ken Menkhaus, "Governance without Government in Somalia: Spoilers, State Building, and the Politics of Coping," *International Security* 31 (Winter 2006/7): 79, fig. 1. *Source*: M. E. J. Newman, "Maps of the 2008 US Presidential Election Results," accessed May 5, 2010, http://www-personal.umich.edu/~mejn /election/2008/. *Source*: "2006 Election Results," House of Representatives map, *Washington Post*, accessed May 5, 2010, http://projects .washingtonpost.com/elections/keyraces /map/. *Source*: Google Maps, map of 1427 E. 60th St., Chicago, IL 60637, accessed May 5, 2010, http://maps.google.com/.

	Short citation	▶ Use full citations for all figures.
	Bibliography	Menkhaus, Ken. "Governance without Government in Somalia: Spoilers, State Building, and the Politics of Coping," *International Security* 31 (Winter 2006/7): 74–106.

▶ Do not include any maps, charts, graphs or tables in the bibliography; *do* include any book, article, or other publication used as the source for such an item. Google Maps does not need to appear in the bibliography; the other sources do.

Newman, M. E. J. "Maps of the 2008 US Presidential Election Results." Accessed May 5, 2010. http://www-personal.umich .edu/~mejn/election/2008/.

"2006 Election Results." *Washington Post,* accessed May 5, 2010. http://projects .washingtonpost.com/elections/keyraces /map/.

Musical recording **First note**

[99] Robert Johnson, "Cross Road Blues," 1937, *Robert Johnson: King of the Delta Blues Singers*, Columbia Records 1654, 1961.

[99] Samuel Barber, "Cello Sonata, for cello and piano, Op. 6," *Barber: Adagio for Strings, Violin Concerto, Orchestral and Chamber Works*, compact disc 2, St. Louis Symphony, cond. Leonard Slatkin, Alan Stepansky (cello), Israela Margalit (piano), EMI Classics 74287, 2001.

[99] Jimi Hendrix, "Purple Haze," 1969, *Woodstock: Three Days of Peace and Music*, compact disc 4 of 4, Atlantic/Wea, 1994.

[99] Vladimir Horowitz, Hungarian Rhapsody no. 2, by Franz Liszt, recorded live at Carnegie Hall, February 25, 1953, MP3 file (241 Kbps).

▶ Kbps stands for kilobits per second; MP3 is the name of the popular audio compression format. If the MP3 file is just a copy of a version from compact disc or LP, you can cite the original:

[99] Vladimir Horowitz, Hungarian Rhapsody no. 2, by Franz Liszt, recorded live at Carnegie Hall, February 25, 1953, compact disc, RCA Victor 60523-2-RG, 1991.

Short note		[99] Johnson, "Cross Road Blues."
		[99] Barber, "Cello Sonata, Op. 6."
		[99] Hendrix, "Purple Haze."
		[99] Horowitz, Hungarian Rhapsody no. 2.
Bibliography		Johnson, Robert. "Cross Road Blues." 1937. *Robert Johnson: King of the Delta Blues Singers.* Columbia Records 1654, 1961.
		Barber, Samuel. "Cello Sonata, for cello and piano, Op. 6." *Barber: Adagio for Strings, Violin Concerto, Orchestral and Chamber Works.* Compact disc 2. St. Louis Symphony. Cond. Leonard Slatkin, Alan Stepansky (cello), Israela Margalit (piano). EMI Classics 74287, 2001.
		Hendrix, Jimi. "Purple Haze," 1969. *Woodstock: Three Days of Peace and Music.* Compact disc 4. Atlantic/Wea, 1994.
		Horowitz, Vladimir. Hungarian Rhapsody no. 2, by Franz Liszt. Recorded live at Carnegie Hall, February 25, 1953. MP3 file (241 Kbps).

Music video, comments on music video	First note	[99] Beyoncé, "Single Ladies (Put a Ring on It)," music video, directed by Jake Nava, released October 13, 2008, MPEG-4.
		[99] Rihanna featuring Jay-Z, "Umbrella," music video, directed by Chris Applebaum, from *Good Girl Gone Bad*, Def Jam, 2007, accessed May 5, 2010, http://www.mtv.com/videos /rihanna/146709/umbrella.jhtml.
		[99] Taylor Swift, "Love Story," music video, 2008, accessed May 5, 2010, http://www.youtube .com/watch?v=z4xmxb9K8RI.
		[99] valeriechic12, comment on "Love Story," by Taylor Swift, music video, October 22, 2009, accessed May 5, 2010, http://www.youtube .com/watch?v=z4xmxb9K8RI.
	Short note	[99] Beyoncé, "Single Ladies."
		[99] Rihanna, "Umbrella."
		[99] Swift, "Love Story."
		[99] valeriechic12, comment on Swift, "Love Story."

	Bibliography	Beyoncé. "Single Ladies (Put a Ring on It)." Music video. Directed by Jake Nava, released October 13, 2008. MPEG-4. Rihanna, featuring Jay-Z. "Umbrella." Music video. Directed by Chris Applebaum. From *Good Girl Gone Bad*. Def Jam, 2007. Accessed May 5, 2010. http://www.mtv.com/videos/rihanna/146709/umbrella.jhtml. Swift, Taylor. "Love Story." Music video, 2008. Accessed May 5, 2010. http://www.youtube.com/watch?v=z4xmxb9K8RI. ▸ Viewers' comments on music videos are not included in bibliographies.
Sheet music	First note	[99] Johann Sebastian Bach, "Toccata and Fugue in D Minor," 1708, BWV 565, arranged by Ferruccio Benvenuto Busoni for solo piano (New York: G. Schirmer LB1629, 1942).
	Short note	[99] Bach, "Toccata and Fugue in D Minor."
	Bibliography	Bach, Johann Sebastian. "Toccata and Fugue in D Minor." 1708. BWV 565. Arranged by Ferruccio Benvenuto Busoni for solo piano. New York: G. Schirmer LB1629, 1942. ▸ This piece was written in 1708 and has the standard Bach classification BWV 565. This particular arrangement was published by G. Schirmer in 1942 and has their catalog number LB1629.
Liner notes	First note	[99] Steven Reich, liner notes for *Different Trains*, Elektra/Nonesuch 9 79176-2, 1988.
	Short note	[99] Reich, liner notes. ▸ Or [99] Reich, liner notes, *Different Trains*.
	Bibliography	Reich, Steven. Liner notes for *Different Trains*. Elektra/Nonesuch 9 79176-2, 1988.
Advertisement, hard copy and online	First note	[99] *Letters from Iwo Jima* advertisement, *New York Times*, February 6, 2007, B4. ▸ You may omit pagination from newspapers,

if you wish, since these vary from edition to edition.

[99] Mercedes-Benz 2007 CL, "Pillarless" advertisement, *New Yorker*, February 12, 2007, 26.

[99] Tab cola, "Be a Mindsticker," television advertisement, ca. late 1960s, accessed May 5, 2010, http://www.dailymotion.com/video /x2s3qi_1960s-tab-commercial-be-a-mindstick _ads.

Short note
[99] *Letters from Iwo Jima* advertisement.
[99] Mercedes-Benz 2007 CL, "Pillarless" advertisement.
[99] Tab advertisement.

Bibliography
▶ Advertisements are rarely included in bibliographies, but you may include them if they are especially important to your work.

Letters from *Iwo Jima* advertisement. *New York Times*, February 6, 2007.

Mercedes-Benz 2007 CL. "Pillarless" advertisement. *New Yorker*, February 12, 2007, 26.

Tab cola. "Be a Mindsticker." Television advertisement, ca. late 1960s. Accessed May 5, 2010. http://www.dailymotion .com/video/x2s3qi_1960s-tab-commercial -be-a-mindstick_ads.

Government document, hard copy and online

First note
[99] Senate Committee on Armed Services, *Hearings on S. 758, A Bill to Promote the National Security by Providing for a National Defense Establishment*, 80th Cong., 1st sess., 1947, S. Rep. 239, 13.

▶ "S. Rep. 239, 13" refers to report number 239, page 13.

[99] *Financial Services and General Government Appropriations Act, 2008*, HR 2829, 110th Cong., 1st sess., *Congressional Record* 153 (June 28, 2007): H7347.

[99] *Financial Services and General Government Appropriations Act, 2008*, HR 2829, 110th Cong., 1st sess., *Congressional Record*

153 (June 28, 2007): H7347, accessed May 5, 2010, http://frwebgate.access.gpo.gov/cgi -bin/getpage.cgi?position=all&page=H7347 &dbname=2007_record.
[99] Environmental Protection Agency (EPA), *Final Rule, Air Pollution Control: Prevention of Significant Deterioration; Approval and Promulgation of Implementation Plans, Federal Register* 68, no. 247 (December 24, 2003): 74483–91.
[99] U.S. Department of State, Daily Press Briefing, September 25, 2009, accessed May 5, 2010, http://www.state.gov/r/pa/prs /dpb/2009/sept/129621.htm.

Short note   [99] Senate, *Hearings on S. 758*, 13.
[99] *Financial Services and General Government Appropriations Act, 2008,* HR 2829, *Cong. Rec.,* (June 28, 2007): H7347.
[99] EPA, *Final Rule, Air Pollution Control.*
[99] U.S. State Department, Daily Press Briefing, September 25, 2009.

Bibliography   U.S. Congress. Senate. Committee on Armed Services. *Hearings on S. 758, Bill to Promote the National Security by Providing for a National Defense Establishment.* 80th Cong., 1st sess., 1947. S. Rep. 239.
U.S. Congress. House. *Congressional Record.* 110th Cong., 1st sess. June 28, 2007. Vol. 153, no. 106. H7347.
U.S. Congress. House. *Congressional Record.* 110th Cong., 1st sess. June 28, 2007. Vol. 153, no. 106. H7347. Accessed May 5, 2010. http://frwebgate.access.gpo.gov/cgi-bin /getpage.cgi?position=all&page=H7347 &dbname=2007_record.
Environmental Protection Agency. *Final Rule, Air Pollution Control: Prevention of Significant Deterioration; Approval and Promulgation of Implementation Plans. Federal Register* 68, no. 247 (December 24, 2003): 74483–91.

U.S. Department of State. Daily Press Briefing. September 25, 2009. Accessed May 5, 2010. http://www.state.gov/r/pa/prs /dpb/2009/sept/129621.htm.

Software	First note	[99] *Dreamweaver CS4 (10.0)* (San Francisco: Adobe, September 23, 2008).
		[99] *iTunes 9.0.1* (Cupertino, CA: Apple, September 22, 2009).
		[99] *Stata 11* (College Station, TX: Stata, July 27, 2009).
		[99] J. Scott Long and Jeremy Freese, *Regression Models for Categorical Dependent Variables Using Stata*, 2nd ed. (College Station, TX: Stata, 2006).
		▸ Long and Freese's book shows how to use Stata software. It is treated like other texts.
	Short note	[99] *Dreamweaver CS4 (10.0)*.
		[99] *iTunes 9.0.1*.
		[99] *Stata 11*.
		[99] Long and Freese, *Regression Models*.
	Bibliography	*Dreamweaver CS4 (10.0)*. San Francisco: Adobe, September 23, 2008.
		iTunes 9.0.1. Cupertino, CA: Apple, September 22, 2009.
		Stata 11. College Station, TX: Stata, July 27, 2009.
		Long, J. Scott, and Jeremy Freese. *Regression Models for Categorical Dependent Variables Using Stata*. 2nd ed. College Station, TX: Stata, 2006.
Database	First note	[99] Corpus Scriptorum Latinorum database of Latin literature, accessed May 5, 2010, http:// www.forumromanum.org/literature/index .html.
		▸ For a specific item within this database:
		[99] Gaius Julius Caesar, *Commentarii de bello civili*, ed. A. G. Peskett (Loeb Classical Library; London: W. Heinemann, 1914), in Corpus

Scriptorum Latinorum database of Latin literature, accessed May 5, 2010, http://www .thelatinlibrary.com/caes.html.

[99] Maryland Department of Assessments and Taxation, Real Property Data Search v2.0, accessed May 5, 2010, http://sdatcert3.resiusa .org/rp_rewrite/.

[99] U.S. Copyright Office, Search Copyright Records, accessed May 5, 2010, http://www .copyright.gov/records/.

[99] United Nations Treaty Collection, Databases, accessed May 5, 2010, http://treaties.un.org/.

▸ For a specific item within this database:

[99] "International Tropical Timber Agreement, 2006 (adopted January 27, 2006)," in United Nations Treaty Collection, Databases, accessed May 5, 2010, http://treaties.un.org/doc /source/RecentTexts/XIX_46_english.pdf.

Short note

[99] Corpus Scriptorum Latinorum.

[99] Caesar, *Commentarii de bello civil*.

[99] Maryland, Real Property Data Search.

[99] U.S. Copyright Office, Search Copyright Records.

[99] United Nations Treaty Collection, Databases.

[99] "International Tropical Timber Agreement, 2006."

Bibliography

Corpus Scriptorum Latinorum. Database of Latin literature. Accessed May 5, 2010. http://www.forumromanum.org/literature /index.html.

Caesar, Gaius Julius. *Commentarii de bello civili*. Edited by A. G. Peskett. Loeb Classical Library. London: W. Heinemann, 1914. In Corpus Scriptorum Latinorum database of Latin literature. Accessed May 5, 2010. http://www.thelatinlibrary.com/caes.html.

Maryland Department of Assessments and Taxation. Real Property Data Search v2.0. Accessed May 5, 2010. http://sdatcert3 .resiusa.org/rp_rewrite/.

U.S. Copyright Office. Search Copyright Records. Accessed May 5, 2010. http:// www.copyright.gov/records/.

United Nations Treaty Collection. Databases.
  Accessed May 5, 2010. http://treaties
  .un.org/.

► For a specific item within this database:

"International Tropical Timber Agreement, 2006
  (adopted January 27, 2006)." In United
  Nations Treaty Collection, Databases.
  Accessed May 5, 2010. http://treaties
  .un.org/doc/source/RecentTexts/XIX_46
  _english.pdf.

Website, entire	First note	[99] Digital History (website), ed. Steven Mintz, accessed May 5, 2010, http://www.digital history.uh.edu/. [99] Internet Public Library (IPL), accessed May 5, 2010, http://www.ipl.org/. [99] Yale University, History Department home page, accessed May 5, 2010, http://www.yale .edu/history/. ► You may omit "home page" if it is obvious.
	Short note	[99] Digital History. [99] Internet Public Library. [99] Yale History Department.
	Bibliography	Digital History (website). Edited by Steven Mintz. Accessed May 5, 2010. http://www .digitalhistory.uh.edu/. Internet Public Library (IPL). Accessed May 5, 2010. http://www.ipl.org/. Yale University. History Department home page. Accessed May 5, 2010. http://www .yale.edu/history/.
Web page, with author	First note	[99] Charles Lipson, "News and Commentary: US and the World," accessed May 5, 2010, http:// www.charleslipson.com/News-links.htm.
	Short note	[99] Lipson, "News and Commentary."
	Bibliography	Lipson, Charles. "News and Commentary: US and the World." Accessed May 5, 2010. http://www.charleslipson.com/News-links .htm.

▶ Include the title or description of the web page if available. That way, if the link changes, it may still be possible to find the page through a search.

Web page, no author	First note	[99] "*I Love Lucy*: Series Summary," Sitcoms Online, accessed May 5, 2010, http://www.sitcomsonline.com/ilovelucy.html.
	Short note	[99] "*I Love Lucy*: Series Summary."
	Bibliography	"*I Love Lucy*: Series Summary." Sitcoms Online. Accessed May 5, 2010. http://www.sitcomsonline.com/ilovelucy.html.
Blog entry or comment	First note	[99] Daniel W. Drezner, "A Dangerous Moment of Foreign Policy Fatigue." *Daniel W. Drezner* (*Foreign Policy* magazine blog), October 29, 2009, accessed May 5, 2010, http://drezner.foreignpolicy.com/posts/2009/10/29/a_dangerous_moment_of_foreign_policy_fatigue.

▶ If this entry had no title, it would be cited as: Daniel W. Drezner, untitled entry, *Daniel W. Drezner* (*Foreign Policy* magazine blog) . . .

[99] Jonathan Adler, "The Roberts Court's Hidden 'Heart of Darkness,'" *The Volokh Conspiracy* (blog), September 28, 2009, accessed May 5, 2010, http://volokh.com/2009/09/.

▶ This is the URL to the archive for September 2009. You can instead list the URL to the article itself (in this case, http://volokh.com/2009/09/28/the-roberts-courts-hidden-heart-of-darkness/).

[99] Hans Bader, September 28, 2009 (12:14 p.m.), comment on Jonathan Adler, "The Roberts Court's Hidden 'Heart of Darkness,'" *The Volokh Conspiracy* (blog), September 28, 2009, accessed May 5, 2010, http://volokh.com/2009/09/28/the-roberts-courts-hidden-heart-of-darkness/#comments.

▶ Hans Bader made more than one comment on this entry so the time is included to specify which one.

Short note	[99] Drezner, "Foreign Policy Fatigue." [99] Adler, "Roberts Court." [99] Bader, comment on "Roberts Court."
Bibliography	▸ Blog items are not usually part of the bibliography, but you may include them if the items are important in their own right or are especially significant for your paper. Here is the format:

Drezner, Daniel W. "A Dangerous Moment of Foreign Policy Fatigue." *Daniel W. Drezner* (*Foreign Policy* magazine blog), October 29, 2009. Accessed May 5, 2010. http://drezner.foreignpolicy.com/posts/2009/10/29/a_dangerous_moment_of_foreign_policy_fatigue.

Adler, Jonathan. "The Roberts Court's Hidden 'Heart of Darkness.'" *The Volokh Conspiracy* (blog), September 28, 2009. Accessed May 5, 2010. http://volokh.com/2009/09/28/the-roberts-courts-hidden-heart-of-darkness/.

Bader, Hans. September 28, 2009 (12:14 p.m.). Comment on Jonathan Adler, "The Roberts Court's Hidden 'Heart of Darkness.'" *The Volokh Conspiracy* (blog), September 28, 2009. Accessed May 5, 2010. http://volokh.com/2009/09/28/the-roberts-courts-hidden-heart-of-darkness/#comments.

Video clip, news video	First note	[99] *Duck and Cover*, Federal Civil Defense Administration/Archer Productions, 1951, video file, posted August 19, 2008, accessed May 5, 2010, http://en.wikipedia.org/wiki/File:DuckandC1951.0gg. [99] "Girl, 9, Drives into Cop Car," CNN video news clip, June 24, 2009, posted August 21, 2009, accessed May 5, 2010, http://www.cnn.com/video/#/video/us/2009/08/21/weakley.tn.child.driver.wkrn.
	Short note	[99] *Duck and Cover*. [99] "Girl, 9, Drives into Cop Car," June 24, 2009.

	Bibliography	*Duck and Cover.* Federal Civil Defense Administration/Archer Productions, 1951. Video file. Posted August 19, 2008. Accessed May 5, 2010. http://en.wikipedia.org/wiki/File:DuckandC1951.ogg. "Girl, 9, Drives into Cop Car." CNN video news clip. June 24, 2009. Posted August 21, 2009. Accessed May 5, 2010. http://www.cnn.com/video/#/video/us/2009/08/21/weakley.tn.child.driver.wkrn.
Video blog (vlog) entry or comment	First note	[99] Steve Garfield, "Vlog Soup 23," Steve Garfield's Video Blog, video posted January 29, 2007, accessed May 5, 2010, http://stevegarfield.blogs.com/videoblog/2007/01/vlog_soup_23.html. [99] Ahmer Zaidi, "Setting a LAMP Test Environment in Ubuntu Linux," video posted August 30, 2009, on Zipke, accessed May 5, 2010, http://zipke.com/2009/08/setting-a-lamp-test-environment-in-ubuntu-linux/. [99] Jatin, October 6, 2009. Comment on "Setting a LAMP Test Environment in Ubuntu Linux," video posted August 30, 2009, accessed May 5, 2010, http://zipke.com/2009/08/setting-a-lamp-test-environment-in-ubuntu-linux/.
	Short note	[99] Garfield, "Vlog Soup 23." [99] Zaidi, "Setting a LAMP Test Environment." [99] Jatin, comment on "Setting a LAMP Test Environment."
	Bibliography	Garfield, Steve. "Vlog Soup 23." Steve Garfield's Video Blog. Video posted January 29, 2007. Accessed May 5, 2010. http://stevegarfield.blogs.com/videoblog/2007/01/vlog_soup_23.html. Zaidi, Ahmer. "Setting a LAMP Test Environment in Ubuntu Linux." Video posted August 30, 2009, on Zipke. Accessed May 5, 2010. http://zipke.com/2009/08/setting-a-lamp-test-environment-in-ubuntu-linux/.

Jatin. October 6, 2009. Comment on "Setting a LAMP Test Environment in Ubuntu Linux." Video posted August 30, 2009. Accessed May 5, 2010. http://zipke.com/2009/08 /setting-a-lamp-test-environment-in -ubuntu-linux/.

Podcast or video podcast (vodcast)	First note	[99] Ferrett Steinmetz, "Suicide Notes, Written by an Alien Mind," *Pseudopod: The Sound of Horror* (podcast), read by Phil Rossi, October 2, 2009, accessed May 5, 2010, http://pseudopod .org/2009/10/02/pseudopod-162-suicide -notes-written-by-an-alien-mind/. [99] "2057: Human Civilization," Discovery Channel, video podcast, December 27, 2006, accessed May 5, 2010, http://dsc.discovery .com/videos/2057-human-civilization.html. ▸ Or [99] Micheo Kaku, host, "2057: Human Civilization," Discovery Channel, video podcast, December 27, 2006, accessed May 5, 2010, http://dsc.discovery.com/videos/2057-human -civilization.html.
	Short note	[99] Steinmetz, "Suicide Notes." [99] "2057: Human Civilization." ▸ Or [99] Kaku, "2057: Human Civilization."
	Bibliography	Steinmetz, Ferrett. "Suicide Notes, Written by an Alien Mind." *Pseudopod: The Sound of Horror* (podcast). Read by Phil Rossi. October 2, 2009. Accessed May 5, 2010. http://pseudopod.org/2009/10/02 /pseudopod-162-suicide-notes-written-by -an-alien-mind/. "2057: Human Civilization." Discovery Channel. Video podcast. December 27, 2006. Accessed May 5, 2010. http://dsc .discovery.com/videos/2057-human -civilization.html. ▸ Or

Kaku, Micheo, host. "2057: Future of Civilization." Discovery Channel. Video podcast. December 27, 2006. Accessed May 5, 2010. http://dsc.discovery.com /videos/2057-human-civilization.html.

Social networking site (Facebook, MySpace, Twitter)	First note	[99] Barney Fife, profile at MySpace, accessed May 5, 2010, http://www.myspace.com /15431304. [99] "Info," on Barack Obama's Facebook page, accessed May 5, 2010, http://www.facebook .com/barackobama. [99] Barack Obama, comment on Facebook, October 20, 2009, 11:31 a.m., accessed May 5, 2010, http://www.facebook .com/barackobama. [99] Shaquille O'Neal, comment on Twitter, October 20, 2009, 1:22 p.m., accessed May 5, 2010, http://twitter.com/THE_REAL_SHAQ.
	Short note	[99] Fife, profile at MySpace. [99] "Info," on Barack Obama's Facebook page. [99] Obama, comment on Facebook, October 20, 2009, 11:31 a.m. [99] O'Neal, comment on Twitter, October 20, 2009, 1:22 p.m.
	Bibliography	▶ Do not include individual comments posted to social networking sites in the bibliography. It is fine, however, to include a particular person's page. Obama, Barack. Facebook page. Accessed May 5, 2010. http://www.facebook.com /barackobama.
E-mail and text messages, instant messages (chat), and electronic mailing lists or discussion groups	First note	[99] Mark Quigley, "National Council on Disability Calls for Health Care Reform for People with Disabilities," e-mail from Mark Quigley to National Council on Disability News List (NCD-NEWS-L), September 30, 2009, http://listserv .access.gpo.gov/. ▶ No access date is required when citing e-mail messages.

► Include the URL if the mass e-mailing has been archived.

[99] Kathy Leis, e-mail message to author, May 5, 2010.

[99] Kathy Leis, text message to author, May 5, 2010.

[99] Michael Lipson, instant message to Jonathan Lipson, May 5, 2010.

► You may include the time of an electronic message if it is important or differentiates it from others. For example:

[99] Michael Lipson, text message to Jonathan Lipson, May 5, 2010, 11:23 a.m.

► Save copies of electronic messages that you intend to cite.

Short note

[99] Mark Quigley to NCD-NEWS-L, September 30, 2009.

[99] Kathy Leis, e-mail message to author, May 3, 2007.

► You may be able to shorten these notes. If you are citing only one person named Leis, for instance, then you can drop the first name. But if you are citing messages from Alan Leis, Kathy Leis, Elizabeth Leis, and Julia Leis, then it is much clearer to include their first names, even in short notes.

[99] Michael Lipson, instant message to Jonathan Lipson, May 5, 2010.

[99] Michael Lipson, text message to Jonathan Lipson, May 5, 2010, 11:23 a.m.

Bibliography

► Personal e-mails, text and other instant messages, and e-mails to mailing lists are not included in the bibliography unless they can be retrieved by third parties.

Quigley, Mark. "National Council on Disability Calls for Health Care Reform for People with Disabilities." E-mail to National Council on Disability News List (NCD-NEWS-L), September 30, 2009. http://listserv.access .gpo.gov/.

CHICAGO: CITATIONS TO TABLES AND NOTES

Citation	Refers to
106	page 106
106n	only note appearing on page 106
107n32	note number 32 on page 107, a page with several notes
89, table 6.2	table 6.2, which appears on page 89; similar for graphs and figures

CHICAGO: COMMON ABBREVIATIONS IN CITATIONS

and others	et al.	edition	ed.	number	no.	pseudonym	pseudo.
appendix	app.	editor	ed.	opus	op.	translator	trans.
book	bk.	especially	esp.	opuses	opp.	versus	vs.
chapter	chap.	figure	fig.	page	p.	volume	vol.
compare	cf.	note	n.	pages	pp.		
document	doc.	notes	nn.	part	pt.		

Note: All abbreviations are lowercase, followed by a period. Most form their plurals by adding "s." The exceptions are note (n. → nn.), opus (op. → opp.), page (p. → pp.), and translator (same abbreviation). (Another exception: when the abbreviation *n.* or *nn.* follows a page number with no intervening space, the period is dropped.)

In citing poetry, do not use abbreviations for "line" or "lines" since a lowercase "l" is easily confused with the number one.

FAQS ABOUT CHICAGO-STYLE CITATIONS

Why do you put the state after some publishers and not after others?
The Chicago Manual of Style recommends using state names for all but the largest, best-known cities. To avoid confusion, they use Cambridge, MA, for Harvard and MIT presses but just Cambridge for Cambridge University Press in the ancient English university town. Also, you can drop the state name if it is already included in the publisher's title, such as Ann Arbor: University of Michigan Press.

What if a book is forthcoming?
Use "forthcoming" just as you would use the year. Here's a bibliographic entry:

Godot, Shlomo. *Still Waiting.* London: Verso, forthcoming.

What if the date or place of publication is missing?
Same idea as "forthcoming." Where you would normally put the place or date, use "n.p." (no place) or "n.d." (no date). For example: (Montreal, QC: McGill-Queen's University Press, n.d.).

What if the author is anonymous or not listed?
Usually, you omit the anonymous author and begin with the title.

If an author is technically anonymous but is actually known, put the name in brackets, as in [Johnson, Samuel] or [Madison, James], and list it wherever the author's name falls.

One book I cite has a title that ends with a question mark. Do I still put periods or commas after it?
Commas, yes; periods, no.

Are notes single-spaced or double-spaced? What about the bibliography?
Space your footnotes and endnotes the same way you do your text.

As for your bibliography, I think it is easiest to read if you single-space within entries and put a double space between the entries. But check what your department or publisher requires. They may require double-spacing for everything.

I'm reading Mark Twain. Do I cite Twain or Samuel Clemens?
When pseudonyms are well known such as Mark Twain or Mother Teresa, you can use them alone, without explanation, if you wish.

If you want to include both the pseudonym and the given name, the rule is simple. Put the better-known name first, followed by the lesser-known one in brackets. It doesn't matter if the "real" name is the lesser-known one.

> George Eliot [Mary Ann Evans]
> Isak Dinesen [Karen Christence Dinesen, Baroness Blixen-Finecke]
> Le Corbusier [Charles-Edouard Jeanneret]
> Benjamin Disraeli [Lord Beaconsfield]
> Lord Palmerston [Henry John Temple]
> Krusty the Clown [Herschel S. Krustofski]

If you wish to include the pseudonym in a bibliographic entry, it reads:

> Aleichem, Sholom [Solomon Rabinovitz]. *Fiddler on the Roof . . .*

Are there any differences between the rules for citations in *The Chicago Manual of Style* and those in Kate L. Turabian's *Manual for Writers of Research Papers, Theses, and Dissertations*?
Turabian's *Manual* is essentially a student version of *The Chicago Manual of Style*. In terms of citation style, the only significant difference between

the two books is that Turabian requires access dates with all citations of online sources, while *The Chicago Manual of Style* considers them optional, depending on the situation. Since this book is intended for students, it follows Turabian's rule and includes access dates.

4 MLA CITATIONS FOR THE HUMANITIES

The Modern Language Association (MLA) has developed a citation style that is widely used in the humanities. Instead of footnotes or endnotes, it uses in-text citations such as (Strier 125). Full information about each item appears in the bibliography, which MLA calls "Works Cited." Like other bibliographies, it contains three essential nuggets of information about each item: the author, title, and publication data. To illustrate, let's use a book by Fouad Ajami. The full entry in the Works Cited is

> Ajami, Fouad. *The Foreigner's Gift: The Americans, the Arabs, and the Iraqis in Iraq*. New York: Free Press, 2006. Print.

What sets MLA style apart is the additional requirement that you include the medium of publication—print, web, e-mail, CD, television, etc.—along with the full facts of publication.

By the way, you may notice that older publications using MLA style underline the title. That was the rule until recently. *Cite Right* is using the latest MLA rules, which use *italics* instead of underlining.

In-text citations are brief and simple. To cite the entire book, just insert (Ajami) at the end of the sentence, or (Ajami 12) to refer to page 12. If your paper happens to cite several books by Ajami, be sure your reader knows which one you are referring to. If that's not clear in the sentence, then include a very brief title: (Ajami, *Gift* 12).

MLA citations can be even briefer—and they should be, whenever possible. They can omit the author and the title as long as it's clear which work is being cited. For example:

> As Ajami notes, these are long-standing problems in Iraqi politics (14–33).

You can omit the in-text reference entirely if the author and title are clear and you are not citing specific pages. For instance:

> Gibbon's *Decline and Fall of the Roman Empire* established new standards of documentary evidence for historians.

In this case, there's nothing to put in an in-text reference that isn't already in the sentence. So, given MLA's consistent emphasis on brevity, you simply skip the reference. You still include Gibbon in your Works Cited.

Because in-text references are so brief, you can string several together in one parenthesis: (Bevington 17; Bloom 75; Vendler 51). The references are separated by semicolons.

If Ajami's book were a three-volume work, then the citation to volume 3, page 17, would be (Ajami 3: 17). If you need to differentiate this work from others by the same author, then include the title: (Ajami, *Gift* 3: 17). If you wanted to cite the volume but not a specific page, then use (Ajami, vol. 3) or (Ajami, *Gift*, vol. 3). Why include "vol." here? So readers won't think you are citing page 3 of a one-volume work.

If several authors have the same last name, simply add their first initials to differentiate them: (C. Brontë, *Jane Eyre*), (E. Brontë, *Wuthering Heights*). Of course, full information about the authors and their works appears at the end, in the Works Cited.

Books like *Jane Eyre* appear in countless editions, and your readers may wish to look up passages in theirs. To make that easier, the MLA recommends that you add some information after the normal page citation. You might say, for example, that the passage appears in chapter 1. For poems, you might note lines or other divisions.

Let's say that you quoted a passage from the first chapter of *Jane Eyre,* which appeared on page 7 in the edition you are using. Insert a semicolon after the page and add the chapter number, using a lowercase abbreviation for chapter: (E. Brontë, *Wuthering Heights* 7; ch. 1). For plays, the act, scene, and lines are separated by periods (*Romeo and Juliet* 1.3.12–15).

When you refer to online documents, there are often no pages to cite. As a substitute, include a section or paragraph number, if there is one. Just put a comma after the author's name, then list the section or paragraph: (Padgett, sec. 9.7) or (Snidal, pars. 12–18). If the online document is a PDF file, go ahead and list the page numbers since those will be the same for all users: (Wang 14). If there's no numbering system, though, just list the author.

In-text citations normally appear at the end of sentences and are followed by the punctuation for the sentence itself. To illustrate:

A full discussion of these issues appears in *Miss Thistlebottom's Hobgoblins* (Bernstein).

In this style, you can still use regular footnotes or endnotes for limited purposes. They can *only* be used for commentary, however, not for citations. If you need to cite some materials within the note itself, use in-text citations there, just as you would in the text.

For brevity—a paramount virtue of the MLA system—the names of publishers are also compressed: Princeton University Press becomes Princeton UP, the University of Chicago Press becomes U of Chicago P. For the same reason, most month names are abbreviated.

MLA's penchant for brevity extends to referencing electronic information—to a point. URLs are no longer required. Instead, just list the medium—usually "Web." For anything that's "Web," you'll also need an access date. So far so good. But for many types of online sources, MLA also requires listing the sponsoring organization. This leads to redundancy. You are supposed to write: *Encyclopaedia Britannica Online.* Encyclopaedia Britannica, 2010 . . . Or *CBSNews.com.* CBS, 5 Mar. 2010 . . . The italicized titles are the works cited; the repeated name is the sponsoring organization. This seems like overkill to me, at least when the sponsoring organization is evident. But that's the current MLA style.

I have provided detailed information and examples in a table below. Because MLA style is often used in the humanities, where citations to plays, poems, paintings, and films are common, I include all of them. If you want still more examples or less common items, consult two useful books published by the MLA:

- *MLA Style Manual and Guide to Scholarly Publishing,* 3rd ed. (New York: Modern Language Association of America, 2008), 163–260.
- *MLA Handbook for Writers of Research Papers,* 7th ed. (New York: Modern Language Association of America, 2009).

They should be available in your library's reference section.

To make it easy to find the citations you need, I've listed them here alphabetically, along with the pages where they are described. At the end of the chapter, I have listed some common MLA abbreviations.

INDEX OF MLA CITATIONS IN THIS CHAPTER

MLA: WORKS CITED AND IN-TEXT CITATIONS

Book, one author	Works Cited	Lipson, Charles. *How to Write a BA Thesis: A Practical Guide from Your First Ideas to Your Finished Paper.* Chicago: U Chicago P, 2005. Print.
		Mavor, Carol. *Reading Boyishly: Roland Barthes, J. M. Barrie, Jacques Henri Lartigue, Marcel Proust, and D. W. Winnicott.* Durham: Duke UP, 2007. Print.
		Robinson, Andrew M. *Multiculturalism and the Foundations of Meaningful Life: Reconciling Autonomy, Identity, and Community.* Vancouver: U of British Columbia P, 2007. Print.

> ► MLA style omits the publisher's state or
> province.

In-text
(Lipson 22–23) or (22–23)
> ► Refers to pages 22–23.
> ► If it is necessary to differentiate this book from
> others by the same author, then cite as:
(Lipson, *BA Thesis* 22–23)
(Mavor 26) or (26)
(Robinson 136) or (136)

Books,
several by
same author

Works Cited
Easterly, William R. *The Elusive Quest for*
Growth: Economists' Adventures and
Misadventures in the Tropics. Cambridge:
MIT P, 2001. Print.
———. *The White Man's Burden: Why the West's*
Efforts to Aid the Rest Have Done So
Much Ill and So Little Good. New York:
Penguin, 2006. Print.
> ► The repetition of the author's name uses three
> hyphens, followed by a period.

In-text
(Easterly, *Elusive* 34; Easterly, *White Man's* 456)

Book,
multiple
authors

Works Cited
Gikandi, Simon, and Evan Mwangi. *The*
Columbia Guide to East African Literature in
English since 1945. New York: Columbia UP,
2007. Print.
Heathcote, Edwin, and Laura Moffatt.
Contemporary Church Architecture.
Hoboken: Wiley, 2007. Print.
Hall, Jacqueline Dowd, et al. *Like a Family: The*
Making of a Southern Cotton Mill World.
Chapel Hill: U of North Carolina P, 1987.
Print.
> ► When there are four or more authors, as there
> are for *Like a Family*, use "et al." after naming the
> first one.

In-text
(Gikandi and Mwangi, *Columbia Guide* 15–26)
or (Gikandi and Mwangi 15–26)
(Heathcote and Moffatt 12)
(Hall et al. 67)

Book, multiple editions	Works Cited	Strunk, William, Jr., and E. B. White. *The Elements of Style*. 50th anniversary ed. New York: Longman, 2009. Print. Gombrich, Richard F. *Theravada Buddhism: A Social History from Ancient Benares to Modern Colombo*. 2nd ed. London: Routledge, 2006. Print. Head, Dominic, ed. *The Cambridge Guide to Literature in English*. 3rd ed. Cambridge: Cambridge UP, 2006. Print. ▸ If this were a multivolume work, then the volume number would come after the edition: 3rd ed. Vol. 2.
	In-text	(Strunk and White 12) (Gombrich 197) (Head 15)
Book, edited	Works Cited	Lutz, John Sutton, ed. *Myth and Memory: Stories of Indigenous-European Contact*. Vancouver: U of British Columbia P, 2007. Print. Waugh, Patricia, ed. *Literary Theory and Criticism: An Oxford Guide*. New York: Oxford UP, 2006. Print. Gilbert, Sandra, and Susan Gubar, eds. *Feminist Literary Theory and Criticism: A Norton Reader*. New York: Norton, 2007. Print.
	In-text	(Lutz 93) (Waugh 72) (Gilbert and Gubar 12)
Book, anonymous or no author	Works Cited	*Through Our Enemies' Eyes: Osama Bin Laden, Radical Islam, and the Future of America*. Washington: Brassey's, 2003. Print. *Golden Verses of the Pythagoreans*. Whitefish: Kessinger, 2003. ▸ Do not use "anonymous" as the author. If the author is unknown, alphabetize by title but ignore any initial article ("a," "an," or "the"). So, *The Holy Koran* is alphabetized under "H."

	In-text	(*Through Our Enemies' Eyes*) (*Golden Verses*)

Book, online and e-books	Works Cited	Dickens, Charles. *Great Expectations.* *1860–61. Project Gutenberg.* Etext 1400. Project Gutenberg, 1998. Web. 5 May 2010. ▸ Project Gutenberg is both the name of the website (italics) and the name of the sponsoring body (not in italics). "Web" says that you cited an Internet source. The date when you access the online content (in this case, 5 May 2010) comes last. Notice that the day comes before the month; that's standard with MLA.
	In-text	(Dickens) ▸ Since this electronic version does not have pagination, cite the chapter numbers. (Dickens, ch. 2)

Multivolume work	Works Cited	Pflanze, Otto. *Bismarck and the Development of Germany.* 3 vols. Princeton: Princeton UP, 1963–90. Print.
	In-text	(Pflanze) or (Pflanze 3: 21) ▸ This refers to volume 3, page 21. (Pflanze, vol. 3) ▸ When a volume is referenced without a specific page, then use "vol." so the volume won't be confused for a page number.

Single volume in a multivolume work	Works Cited	Pflanze, Otto. *The Period of Fortification, 1880– 1898.* Princeton: Princeton UP, 1990. Print. Vol. 3 of *Bismarck and the Development of Germany.* 3 vols. 1963–90. Iriye, Akira. *The Globalizing of America.* Cambridge: Cambridge UP, 1993. Print. Vol. 3 of *Cambridge History of American Foreign Relations.* Ed. Warren I. Cohen. 4 vols. 1993.

▸ Because these volumes have their own titles, MLA does not require the information for the other volumes. If you want, just cite the single title, with no volume number:

Pflanze, Otto. *The Period of Fortification, 1880–1898.* Princeton: Princeton UP, 1990. Print.

Iriye, Akira. *The Globalizing of America.* Cambridge: Cambridge UP, 1993. Print.

| | In-text | (Pflanze) |
| | | (Iriye) |

Reprint of earlier edition	Works Cited	Barzun, Jacques. *Simple and Direct: A Rhetoric for Writers.* 1985. Chicago: U of Chicago P, 1994. Print.
		Smith, Adam. *An Inquiry into the Nature and Causes of the Wealth of Nations.* 1776. Ed. Edwin Cannan. Chicago: U of Chicago P, 1976. Print.
	In-text	(Barzun, *Simple*) or (Barzun)
		(Smith, *Wealth of Nations*) or (Smith)

| Translated volume | Works Cited | Weber, Max. *The Protestant Ethic and the Spirit of Capitalism.* 1904–5. Trans. Talcott Parsons. New York: Scribner's, 1958. Print. |
| | | Tocqueville, Alexis de. *Democracy in America.* Ed. J. P. Mayer. Trans. George Lawrence. New York: Harper, 2000. Print. |

▸ Editor and translator are listed in the order in which they appear on the book's title page.

Beowulf: A New Verse Translation. Trans. Seamus Heaney. New York: Farrar, 2000. Print.

▸ *Beowulf* is an anonymous poem. The translator's name normally comes after the title. But there is an exception. If you wish to comment on the translator's work, then place the translator's name first. For example:

Heaney, Seamus, trans. *Beowulf: A New Verse Translation.* New York: Farrar, 2000. Print.

Parsons, Talcott, trans. *The Protestant Ethic and the Spirit of Capitalism.* By Max Weber. 1904–5. New York: Scribner's, 1958. Print.

	In-text	(Weber, *Protestant Ethic*) or (Weber) (Tocqueville, *Democracy in America*) or (Tocqueville) (Heaney, *Beowulf*) or (*Beowulf*) (Parsons)
Chapter in edited book	Works Cited	Epstein, Leslie. "The Roar of the Crowd." *Scoring from Second: Writers on Baseball.* Ed. Philip F. Deaver. Lincoln: Bison, 2007. 99–103. Print.
	In-text	(Epstein 100)
Journal article, one author	Works Cited	Egan, Shannon. " 'Yet in a Primitive Condition': Edward S. Curtiss's North American Indian." *American Art* 20.3 (2006): 58–83. Print. Leonard, Miriam. "Oedipus in the Accusative: Derrida and Levinas." *Comparative Literature Studies* 43.3 (2006): 224–51. Print. ▸ Refers to volume 43, number 3. ▸ Most scholarly journals are paginated consecutively throughout a year, so including volume, issue number, and year is usually more than sufficient. But if each issue starts over with page 1, including the month or season can be helpful: *American Art* 20.3 (Fall 2006): 58–83.
	In-text	(Egan) or (Egan 64) (Leonard) or (Leonard 226) or (Leonard, "Oedipus" 226). ▸ The title may be needed to differentiate this article from others by the same author.
Journal article, multiple authors	Works Cited	Prendergast, Catherine, and Nancy Abelmann. "Alma Mater: College, Kinship, and the Pursuit of Diversity." *Social Text* 24.1 (Spring 2006): 37–53. Print. ▸ If there are four or more authors: Prendergast, Catherine, et al.

| In-text | (Prendergast and Abelmann 41–42) |

| Journal article, online | Works Cited | Scott, Gray. "Signifying Nothing? A Secondary Analysis of the Claremont Authorship Debates." *Early Modern Literary Studies* 12.2 (Sept. 2006): 6.1–50. Web. 5 May 2010. |

▸ MLA does not require a URL, but if your professor does, include it like this:

Scott, Gray. "Signifying Nothing? A Secondary Analysis of the Claremont Authorship Debates." *Early Modern Literary Studies* 12.2 (Sept. 2006): 6.1–50. Web. 5 May 2010. <http://purl.oclc.org/emls/12–2/scotsig2.htm>.

▸ This online-only journal doesn't have page numbers, but it does include article and paragraph numbers; 6.1–50 means the sixth article, which includes fifty numbered paragraphs. (If there are no such numbers available, use the abbreviation "n. pag." in place of page numbers.) The rest of the citation is the same as a normal print journal except for the addition of the medium ("Web") and an access date (5 May 2010).

Baggetun, Rune, and Barbara Wasson. "Self-Regulated Learning and Open Writing." *European Journal of Education* 41.3–4 (2006): 453–72. *Blackwell Journals Online.* Web. 13 Feb. 2007.

▸ This is a normal print journal, available online from multiple sources such as JSTOR, with the same pagination as the print version. Here I list it through Blackwell Journals Online. MLA italicizes the name of the database, which is followed by "Web" and an access date.

Clark, Michael, et al. "Use of Preferred Music to Reduce Emotional Distress and Symptom Activity During Radiation Therapy." *Journal of Music Therapy* 43.3 (2006): 247–65. *IIMP Full Text/ProQuest.* Web. 5 May 2010.

▸ There are four or more authors in this case, so only the first is listed, followed by "et al."

	In-text	(Scott) or (Scott 6.22) or (Scott, "Signifying Nothing," par. 22) (Baggetun and Wasson) (Clark et al. 247–65)

Journal article, foreign language	Works Cited	Joosten, Jan. "Le milieu producteur du Pentateuque grec." *Revue des Études Juives* 165.3–4 (juillet–décembre 2006): 349–61. Print.
	In-text	(Joosten) or (Joosten 356)

Newspaper or magazine article, no author, hard copy and online	Works Cited	"State Senator's Indictment Details Demands on Staff." *New York Times* 11 Feb. 2007: 23. Print. ▸ This refers to page 23. "Jacopo Tintoretto: A Tribute Well Earned." *Economist* 10–16 Feb. 2007: 90. Print. ▸ The same article online: "Jacopo Tintoretto: A Tribute Well Earned." *Economist.com*. Economist, 8 Feb. 2007. Web. 5 May 2010. ▸ The first date refers to the article, the second to the day it was accessed. ▸ *Economist.com* is the name of the website; Economist is the sponsoring body. (Yes, it's redundant, but those are the MLA style rules.)
	In-text	("State Senator's Indictment" 23) ("Jacopo Tintoretto" 90) ("Jacopo Tintoretto")

Newspaper or magazine article, with author, hard copy and online	Works Cited	Halbfinger, David M. "Politicians Are Doing Hollywood Star Turns." *New York Times* 6 Feb. 2007, natl. ed.: B1+. Print. ▸ The plus sign indicates that the article continues, but not on the next page (this one continues on B7). If the article continued on B2 and ran to B3, you'd write B1–B3. Pinsky, Robert. "Poet's Choice." *Washington Post*. Washington Post, 17 Feb. 2008. Web. 5 May 2010.

> ► The first date refers to the article, the second to the day it was accessed.
> ► Again, for newspapers or magazines consulted online, include the title of the website (e.g., *Washington Post*) and the name of the sponsoring body (Washington Post)—no matter how redundant that might seem.

	In-text	(Halbfinger B7) or (Halbfinger, "Politicians" B7) if you cite more than one article by this author. (Pinsky) or (Pinsky, "Poet's Choice")

Review, hard copy and online	Works Cited	Lane, Joseph H. Rev. of *A Kinder, Gentler America: Melancholia and the Mythical 1950s*, by Mary Caputi. *Perspectives on Politics* 4 Dec. 2006: 749–50. Print. Macintyre, Ben. "Midnight's Grandchildren." Rev. of *In Spite of the Gods: The Strange Rise of Modern India*, by Edward Luce. *New York Times Book Review* 4 Feb. 2007: 16. Print. ► The same review online: Macintyre, Ben. "Midnight's Grandchildren." Rev. of *In Spite of the Gods: The Strange Rise of Modern India*, by Edward Luce. *New York Times*. New York Times, 4 Feb. 2007. Web. 5 May 2010. ► The first date refers to the article, the second to the day it was accessed. ► *New York Times* is the name of the website; New York Times is the sponsor.
	In-text	(Lane 749) or (Lane, "Kinder, Gentler" 749) (Macintyre 16) or (Macintyre, "Midnight's Grandchildren" 16)

Unpublished paper, thesis, or dissertation	Works Cited	Leeds, Ashley. "Interests, Institutions, and Foreign Policy Consistency." Paper presented at the Program on International Politics, Economy, and Security, U Chicago, 15 Feb. 2007. Print. Noble, Lance. "One Goal, Multiple Strategies: Engagement in Sino-American WTO Accession Negotiations." MA thesis. U British Columbia, 2006. Print.

Talmi, Deborah. "The Role of Attention and
Organization in Emotional Memory
Enhancement." Diss. U Toronto, 2006. Print.

	In-text	(Leeds)
		(Noble)
		(Talmi)

Abstract	Works Cited	Tyler, Tom. "Snakes, Skins and the Sphinx: Nietzsche's Ecdysis." *Journal of Visual Culture* 5.3 (2006): 365–85. Abstract. *Sage Journals Online*. Web. 5 May 2010.
		Hatchard, John. "Combating Transnational Crime in Africa: Problems and Perspectives." *Journal of African Law* 50 (Oct. 2006): 145–60. *African Studies Abstracts Online* 17, Abstract No. 21 (2007): 28. Web. 5 May 2010.
	In-text	(Tyler)
		(Hatchard 145–60)

Microfilm, microfiche	Works Cited	Abbott, Alice Irving. *Circumstantial Evidence*. New York: W. B. Smith, 1882. Microform. *American Fiction, 1774–1910*. Reel A-1. Woodbridge: Gale/Primary Source Microfilm, 1998.
		King, Martin Luther, Jr., *FBI file*. Ed. David J. Garrow. Microform. 16 reels. Frederick: U Publications of Am., 1984.
	In-text	(Abbott) To cite page 13 on reel A-1, use (Abbott A-1: 13)
		(King) To cite reel 2, page 12, use (King 2: 12)

| Archival materials and manuscript collections, hard copy or online | Works Cited | Franklin, Isaac. Letter to R. C. Ballard. 28 Feb. 1831. MS. Series 1.1, folder 1. Rice Ballard Papers. Southern Historical Collection. Wilson Lib. U of North Carolina, Chapel Hill. |
| | | Lamson, Mary Swift. "An Account of the Beginning of the B.Y.W.C.A." MS. Boston YWCA Papers. Schlesinger Lib. Radcliffe Institute for Advanced Study, Harvard U. Cambridge, MA. 1891. |

▸ Manuscript is abbreviated "MS." Typescript is "TS." MLA considers these to be like "Print" or "Web" in the other types of citations. Spell out descriptive terms such as "notebook" and "unpublished essay."

Szold, Henrietta. Letter to Rose Jacobs. 3 Feb. 1932. Microform. Reel 1, book 1. Rose Jacobs–Alice L. Seligsberg Collection. Judaica Microforms. Brandeis Lib. Waltham, MA.

Szold, Henrietta. Letter to Rose Jacobs. 9 Mar. 1936. MS. A/125/112. Central Zionist Archives, Jerusalem.

Taraval, Sigismundo. "Journal Recounting Indian Uprisings in Baja California." 1734–1737. MS. Edward E. Ayer Manuscript Collection No. 1240, Newberry Lib. Chicago, IL.

Taft, Horatio Nelson. Diary. Vol. 1, Jan. 1, 1861–Apr. 11, 1862. *American Memory*. Lib. of Congress. Web. 5 May 2010.

In-text

(Franklin) or (Franklin to Ballard) or (Franklin to Ballard, 28 Feb. 1831)

(Lamson) or (Lamson 2)

(Szold) or (Szold to Jacobs) or (Szold to Jacobs, 3 Feb. 1932)

(Szold) or (Szold to Jacobs) or (Szold to Jacobs, 9 Mar. 1936)

(Taraval) or (Taraval, par. 23)

▸ This manuscript uses paragraph numbers, not pages.

(Taft) or (Taft 149)

Encyclopedia, hard copy and online

Works Cited

"African Art." *Encyclopaedia Britannica*. 15th ed. 1987. 13: 134–80. Print.

▸ Alphabetize by the first significant word in title.

▸ Volume and page numbers are optional.

▸ Edition and year are required, but you can omit the city and publisher for well-known encyclopedias, dictionaries, and other references.

"African Art." *Encyclopaedia Britannica Online.*
Encyclopaedia Britannica, 2007. Web. 5
May 2010.
▸ Why does the name, *Encyclopaedia Britannica,*
appear twice? Because it is both the publication
and the "sponsoring organization," and MLA
rules currently require that you list both.
Zangwill, Nick. "Aesthetic Judgment." *Stanford*
Encyclopedia of Philosophy. Metaphysics
Research Lab, Stanford University, 2003;
rev. 2007. Web. 5 May 2010.
▸ This article was originally published online in
2003 and substantially revised in 2007. Both
dates are included.

In-text	("African Arts" 13: 137)
	("Art, African")
	(Zangwill)

Reference book, hard copy and online	Works Cited	Pendergast, Sara, and Tom Pendergast, eds. *Reference Guide to World Literature.* 3rd ed. 2 vols. Detroit: St. James P, 2003. Print.

Cannon, John, ed. *Oxford Companion to British*
History. New York: Oxford UP, 2002. *Oxford*
Reference Online. Web. 5 May 2010.
▸ This book appeared in print in 2002 and was cited
online; the citation includes the information
about the printed book followed by the name
of the database or website.
Cicioni, Mirna. "The periodic table (Il sistema
periodico), prose by Primo Levi, 1975."
Reference Guide to World Literature. Ed.
Sara Pendergast and Tom Pendergast.
3rd ed. 2 vols. Detroit: St. James P, 2003. 2:
1447. Print.
"Napoleon I." *S-9.com: Biographical*
Dictionary. S-9, 2007. Web. 5 May 2010.

In-text	(Pendergast and Pendergast)
	(Cannon)
	(Cicioni 2: 1447)
	("Napoleon I")

Dictionary, hard copy, online, and CD-ROM	Works Cited	"Historiography." *Merriam-Webster's Collegiate Dictionary*. 11th ed. 2003. Print. ▸ You can omit the publisher information. The same entry online: "Historiography." *Merriam-Webster's Online Dictionary*. Merriam Webster, 2010. Web. 5 May 2010. "Protest, *v*." *Compact Edition of the Oxford English Dictionary*. 1971 ed. 2: 2335. Print. ▸ The word "protest" is both a noun and a verb, and I am citing the verb here. "Pluck, *n*." Def. 1. *Oxford English Dictionary*. Ed. J. A. Simpson and E. S. C. Weiner. 2nd ed. Oxford: Clarendon P, 1989. *OED Online*. Web. 5 May 2010. ▸ There are two separate entries for the noun "pluck," and I am citing the first, hence "*n*. Def. 1." The second is for an obscure fish. ▸ The "pluck" citation is to the online edition of the *OED* but lists first the information for the printed edition on which it is based. This is optional. You could also do this: "Pluck, *n*." Def. 1. *Oxford English Dictionary Online*. Oxford: Oxford UP, 2010. Web. 5 May 2010. "Citation." *American Heritage Dictionary of the English Language*. 4th ed. Boston: Houghton, 2000. CD-ROM. "Merci." *Le Nouveau Petit Robert–Dictionnaire de la Langue Française, 2007*. Nouvelle ed. Paris: Le Robert, 2006. Print.
	In-text	("Historiography") or (*Merriam-Webster's Collegiate Dict.*) ("Protest" 2: 2335) or (*Compact OED* 2: 2335) ("Pluck") or (*OED Online*) ("Citation") or (*American Heritage Dict.*) ("Merci") or (*Le Nouveau Petit Robert*)
Bible, Koran (Qur'an)	Works Cited	*Tanakh: The Holy Scriptures: The New JPS Translation according to the Traditional Hebrew Text*. Philadelphia: Jewish Publication Society, 1985. Print.

▸ The Bible, Koran, and other sacred texts do *not* usually appear in Works Cited unless you need to cite a particular version or translation.

In-text   (*Tanakh*, Genesis 1.1, 1.3–5, 2.4), then Genesis 1.1, 1.3–5, 2.4.
▸ Books may be abbreviated, such as Gen. 1.1, 1.3–5, 2.4.
▸ Abbreviations for the next four books are Ex., Lev., Num., and Deut. Abbreviations for other books are easily found with a web search for "abbreviations + Bible."
Koran 18.65–82.

Speech, academic talk, or course lecture	Works Cited	Herman, (Chancellor) Richard. Speech at Dr. Martin Luther King Jr. Community Celebration. U of Illinois, Urbana-Champaign. 14 Jan. 2007. Address. MacFarlane, Seth. "Class Day Speech." Harvard U, Cambridge, MA. Video [pt. 3 of 4]. *YouTube*. YouTube, 8 June 2006. Web. 5 May 2010. ▸ Though MLA does not require URLs, they can be helpful for sources like this one. You would include it like this: MacFarlane, Seth. "Class Day Speech." Harvard U, Cambridge, MA. Video [pt. 3 of 4]. *YouTube*. YouTube, 8 June 2006. Web. 5 May 2010. <http://www.youtube .com/watch?v=gLt73xSJlAM>. Hearn, Maxwell K. "How to Read (and Teach) Chinese Art." Speech to annual convention of the National Art Education Association. New York. 16 Mar. 2007. Address. Doniger, Wendy. Course on evil in Hindu mythology. U of Chicago. 15 Mar. 2007. Lecture.
	In-text	(Herman) (MacFarlane) (Hearn) (Doniger)

Personal communication or interview	Works Cited	Coetzee, J. M. Personal interview. 8 Dec. 2009. Sarkozy, Nicolas. Telephone interview. 5 May 2010. Lucas, George. Video interview (Internet/Skype). 5 May 2010. Anonymous U.S. Marine, recently returned from Afghanistan. Personal interview. 5 May 2010. MacMillan, Margaret. Interview by Kenneth Whyte. "On Her New Book, *Nixon in China: The Week That Changed the World.*" *Macleans* 27 Sept. 2006. *McCleans.ca.* Web. 5 May 2010. Rosenquist, James. Interview by Jan van der Marck. "Reminiscing on the Gulf of Mexico: A Conversation with James Rosenquist." *American Art* 20.3 (Fall 2006): 84–107. Print.
	In-text	(Coetzee) (Sarkozy) (Lucas) (anonymous U.S. Marine) (MacMillan) (Rosenquist 93)
Poem, in print or online	Works Cited	Auden, W. H. "The Shield of Achilles." 1952. *Collected Poems.* Ed. Edward Mendelson. New York: Random, 2007. 596–98. Print. ▸ Auden's poem is dated 1952 by Mendelson. The original date of a poem in a collection or anthology is optional. Bishop, Elizabeth. "The Fish." *The Complete Poems, 1927–1979.* New York: Noonday P/Farrar, 1983. 42–44. Print. Lowell, Robert. "For the Union Dead." *The Top 500 Poems.* Ed. William Harmon. New York: Columbia UP, 1992. 1061–63. Print.

Yeats, W. B. "The Lake Isle of Innisfree." 1892. *Poets.org*. Academy of American Poets, n.d. Web. 5 May 2010.

▸ This indicates Yeats's poem was written in 1892 and is posted on Poets.org, which is run by the Academy of American Poets. The site does not indicate exactly when this poem was posted (hence "n.d."), but it was accessed for this citation on May 5, 2010.

In-text

(Auden 596) or (Auden, "Shield of Achilles" 596) or ("Shield of Achilles" 596) or (Auden 596; lines 9–11) or (Auden, lines 9–11) or (lines 9–11) or (9–11)

▸ Do not use abbreviations for "line" or "lines" since a lowercase "l" is easily confused with the number one.

(Bishop 43) or (Bishop, "The Fish" 43) or ("The Fish" 43) or (43)

(Lowell 1061–63) or (Lowell, "Union Dead" 1061–63)

(Yeats) or (Yeats, "Innisfree")

Play, text

Works Cited

Bunin, Keith. *The Busy World Is Hushed*. 2006. New York: Dramatists Play Service, 2007. Print.

▸ The play was written in 2006, published in 2007.

Shakespeare, William. *Romeo and Juliet*.

▸ If you wish to cite a specific edition, then:

Shakespeare, William. *Romeo and Juliet*. Ed. Brian Gibbons. London: Methuen, 1980. Print.

▸ For an online version:

Shakespeare, William. *Romeo and Juliet*. *Project Gutenberg*. E-text 1112. Project Gutenberg, 1997. Web. 5 May 2010.

In-text

(Bunin) or (Bunin, *Busy World*)

(Shakespeare, *Romeo and Juliet* 1.3.12–15) or (*Romeo and Juliet* 1.3.12–15) or (1.3.12–15) if the play's name is clear in the text.

▸ This refers to act 1, scene 3, lines 12–15 (separated by periods).

▶ If you refer repeatedly to Shakespeare's plays, you can use MLA's standard abbreviations for them, such as (*Ham.*) for *Hamlet.* The first time you mention a play such as *Romeo and Juliet,* you simply indicate the abbreviation (*Rom.*), and then use it after that for in-text citations, such as (*Rom.* 1.3.12–15).

Performance of play or dance	Works Cited	*Bitter Suite.* Chor. Jorma Elo. Music Felix Mendelssohn and Claudio Monteverdi. Hubbard Street Dance Chicago. Harris Theater for Music and Dance at Millennium Park, Chicago. 2 Oct. 2009. Performance.

Fake. Writ. and dir. Eric Simonson. Perf. Kate Arrington, Francis Guinan, and Alan Wilder, Steppenwolf Theatre, Chicago, 28 Oct. 2009. Performance.

▶ If you are concentrating on one person's work in theater, music, dance, or other collaborative arts, put that person's name first. For example, if you are focusing on Kate Arrington's acting:

Arrington, Kate, perf. *Fake.* Writ. and dir. Eric Simonson . . .

▶ If, by contrast, you are focusing on Eric Simonson's writing and directing or on (writing and) directing in general:

Simonson, Eric, writ. and dir. *Fake.* Perf. Kate Arrington, . . .

	In-text	(*Bitter Suite*)

(*Fake*) or (Arrington) or (Simonson)

Television program	Works Cited	"Bart vs. Lisa vs. 3rd Grade." Writ. T. Long. Dir. S. Moore. *The Simpsons.* Fox. 17 Nov. 2002. Television.

"Into the Crevasse." Dir. Beth McCarthy Miller. *30 Rock.* NBC. 22 Oct. 2009. *Hulu.* Web. 17 Nov. 2009.

▶ The first date is the original broadcast date on NBC; the second date is when it was watched on Hulu.

	In-text	("Bart vs. Lisa") ("Into the Crevasse")
Film	Works Cited	*Godfather II*. Dir. Francis Ford Coppola. Perf. Al Pacino, Robert De Niro, Robert Duvall, Diane Keaton. Screenplay by Francis Ford Coppola and Mario Puzo based on the novel by Mario Puzo. Paramount Pictures, 1974. Paramount Home Video, Godfather DVD Collection, 2003. DVD. ▸ Required: title, director, distributor/studio, and year released. Include them, or you will sleep with the fishes. ▸ Optional: actors, producers, screenwriters, editors, cinematographers, and other information. Include what you need for analysis in your paper, in order of their importance to your analysis. Their names appear between the title and the distributor. ▸ If you are concentrating on one person's work, put that person's name and role (such as performer) first, before the title: Coppola, Francis Ford, dir. *Godfather II*. Perf. Al Pacino, Robert De Niro, Robert Duvall, Diane Keaton. Paramount Pictures, 1974. Paramount Home Video, Godfather DVD Collection, 2003. DVD.
	In-text	(*Godfather II*)
Artwork, original	Works Cited	Tintoretto, Jacopo Robusti. *The Birth of John the Baptist*. 1550s. Oil on canvas, 181 × 266 cm. Hermitage, St. Petersburg. ▸ The size is optional.
	In-text	(Tintoretto) or (Tintoretto, *Birth of John the Baptist*)
Artwork, reproduction	Works Cited	Tintoretto, Jacopo Robusti. *The Birth of John the Baptist*. 1550s. Hermitage, St. Petersburg. *Tintoretto: Tradition and Identity*. By Tom Nichols. London: Reaktion Books, 1999. 47. Print.

	In-text	(Tintoretto) or (Tintoretto, *Birth of John the Baptist*)

Artwork, online	Works Cited	Tintoretto, Jacopo Robusti. *The Birth of John the Baptist*. 1550s. Hermitage, St. Petersburg. *State Hermitage Museum*. Web. 5 May 2010. Tintoretto, Jacopo Robusti. *The Birth of John the Baptist* (detail). 1550? Hermitage, St. Petersburg. *CGFA*. Web. 5 May 2010. ▸ The same artwork accessed through the museum's site and another site.
	In-text	(Tintoretto) or (Tintoretto, *Birth of John the Baptist*)

Photograph, original	Works Cited	Adams, Ansel. *Monolith, the Face of Half Dome, Yosemite National Park*. 1927. Photograph. Art Institute, Chicago.
	In-text	(Adams) or (Adams, *Monolith*)

Photograph, online	Works Cited	Adams, Ansel. *Dunes, Oceano*. 1963. *Ansel Adams Gallery*. Web. 5 May 2010.
	In-text	(Adams) or (Adam, *Dunes, Oceano*)

Figures: map, chart, graph, or table	Works Cited	"Climate Change Vulnerability in Africa." Map. *UNEP/GRID-Arendal Maps and Graphics Library*. UNEP/GRID-Arendal, 2002, updated 2004, 2005. Web. 5 May 2010. "House of Representatives, 2006 Election Results." Map. *Washington Post*. Washington Post, n.d. Web. 5 May 2010. "1427 E. 60th St., Chicago IL 60637." Map. *Google Maps*. Google, 2010. Web. 5 May 2010. ▸ MLA treats maps like anonymous books. "Map of Somalia, 2006." Map. "Governance without Government in Somalia: Spoilers, State Building, and the Politics of Coping." By Ken Menkhaus. *International Security* 31 (Winter 2006/7): 79. Print.

▶ Or

Menkhaus, Ken. "Governance without
  Government in Somalia: Spoilers, State
  Building, and the Politics of Coping."
  International Security 31 (Winter 2006/7):
  74–106. Print.

In-text   ("Climate Change Vulnerability in Africa")
  ("House of Representatives, 2006" map)
  ("Map of Somalia, 2006/7") or (Menkhaus 79,
  map)

Musical   Works Cited   Johnson, Robert. "Come On in My Kitchen
recording   (Take 1)." Rec. 23 Nov. 1936. *Robert
                              Johnson: King of the Delta Blues
                              Singers*. Expanded ed. Columbia/
                              Legacy CK 65746, 1998. CD.
                           Johnson, Robert. "Traveling Riverside Blues."
                              Rec. 20 June 1937. *Robert Johnson: King of
                              the Delta Blues Singers*. Columbia Records
                              1654, 1961. LP.
                           Allman Brothers Band. "Come On in My
                              Kitchen." By Robert Johnson. *Shades of
                              Two Worlds*. Sony, 1991. CD.
                           Barber, Samuel. Cello sonata, for cello and
                              piano, op. 6. *Barber: Adagio for Strings,
                              Violin Concerto, Orchestral and Chamber
                              Works*. Disc 2. St. Louis Symphony. Cond.
                              Leonard Slatkin. Cello, Alan Stepansky.
                              Piano, Israela Margalit. EMI Classics 74287,
                              2001. CD.
                           ▶ The catalog numbers are optional but helpful.
                           ▶ If you are concentrating on one person's work,
                              such as the pianist, his or her name can come
                              first:
                           Margalit, Israela, piano. Cello sonata, for
                              cello and piano, op. 6. *Barber: Adagio
                              for Strings, Violin Concerto, Orchestral
                              and Chamber Works*. Disc 2. St. Louis
                              Symphony. Cond. Leonard Slatkin. Cello,
                              Alan Stepansky. EMI Classics 74287, 2001.

		Horowitz, Vladimir, perf. Hungarian Rhapsody no. 2. By Franz Liszt. Rec. live at Carnegie Hall, 25 Feb. 1953. RCA Victor, 1991. MP3 file.
	In-text	(Johnson) or (Johnson, "Come On in My Kitchen") (Johnson) or (Johnson, "Traveling Riverside Blues") (Allman Brothers) or (Allman Brothers, "Come On in My Kitchen") (Barber) or (Barber, Cello sonata) (Margalit) or (Margalit, Cello sonata) (Horowitz) or (Horowitz, Hungarian Rhapsody no. 2)
Music video, comments on music video	Works Cited	Beyoncé. "Single Ladies (Put a Ring on It)." Music video. Dir. Jake Nava. 13 Oct. 2008. MPEG-4 file. Rihanna, featuring Jay-Z. "Umbrella." Music video. Dir. Chris Applebaum. *Good Girl Gone Bad*, Def Jam, 2007. *MTV Networks*. Web. 5 May 2010. Swift, Taylor. "Love Story." Music video. *YouTube*. YouTube, 2008. Web. 5 May 2010. valeriechic12. Comment on "Love Story," by Taylor Swift. Music video. *YouTube*. YouTube, 22 Oct. 2009. Web. 5 May 2010.
	In-text	(Beyoncé) (Rihanna) (Swift) (valeriechic12)
Sheet music	Works Cited	Bach, Johann Sebastian. *Toccata and Fugue in D Minor*. 1708. BWV 565. Arr. Ferruccio Benvenuto Busoni for solo piano. New York: G. Schirmer LB1629, 1942. Print. ▶ This piece was written in 1708 and has the standard Bach classification BWV 565. The arrangement is published by G. Schirmer, with their catalog number LB1629.

	In-text	(*Toccata and Fugue in D Minor*) or (Bach, *Toccata and Fugue in D Minor*)
Liner notes	Works Cited	Reich, Steven. Liner notes. *Different Trains*. Kronos Quartet. Elektra/Nonesuch 9 79176–2, 1988. CD.
	In-text	(Reich, *Different Trains*)
Advertise- ment, hard copy and online	Works Cited	*Letters from Iwo Jima* (film). Advertisement. *New York Times* 6 Feb. 2007: B4. Print. Mercedes-Benz 2007 CL-class automobiles. Advertisement. *New Yorker* 12 Feb. 2007: 26. Print. Tab cola. "Be a Mindsticker." Advertisement. Coca-Cola Co., ca. late 1960s. Television. *Dailymotion*, 2007. Web. 5 May 2010. <http://www.dailymotion.com/video /x2s3qi_1960s-tab-commercial-be-a -mindstick_ads>. ▸ The URL is included because more than one version of the Tab TV ad is posted at *Dailymotion*.
	In-text	(*Letters from Iwo Jima* advertisement) (Mercedes-Benz advertisement) (Tab advertisement)
Government document, hard copy and online	Works Cited	*Cong. Rec.* 21 Oct. 2009: H11519–82. Print. *Cong. Rec.* 21 Oct. 2009: H11519–82. *GPO Access.* Web. 5 May 2010. United States. Cong. Senate. Committee on Armed Services. *Hearings on S. 758, a Bill to Promote the National Security by Providing for a National Defense Establishment.* 80th Cong., 1st sess. S. Rept. 239. Washington: GPO, 1947. Print. Freedman, Stephen. *Four-Year Impacts of Ten Programs on Employment Stability and Earnings Growth: The National Evaluation of Welfare-to-Work Strategies.* Washington: U.S. Department of Education, 2000. EDRS No. ED450262. *ERIC.* Web. 5 May 2010.

United States. Dept. of State. *Daily Press Briefing*. 12 Feb. 2007. *U.S. Department of State*. Web. 5 May 2010.

In-text

(*Cong. Rec.* 21 Oct. 2009: H11523)
(U.S. Cong., Senate, Committee on Armed Services)
▸ If you are only referencing one item from that committee, then in-text citations don't need to include the hearing number or report.
(U.S. Cong., Senate, Committee on Armed Services, *Hearings on S. 758*, 1947)
▸ If you refer to several items from the committee, indicate which one you are citing. You can shorten that after the first use:
(*Hearings on S. 758*)
(Freedman) or (Freedman, *Four-Year Impacts*)
(U.S. Dept. of State) or (U.S. Dept. of State, *Press Briefing*, 12 Feb. 2007)

Software   Works Cited

Dreamweaver CS4 (10.0). San Francisco: Adobe, 2008. Software.
iTunes 9.0.1. Cupertino, CA: Apple, 2009. Software.

In-text

(*Dreamweaver CS4*)
(*iTunes 9.0.1*)

Database   Works Cited

Internet Movie Database (IMDb). Internet Movie Database. Web. 5 May 2010.
Corpus Scriptorum Latinorum. Database of Latin literature. Forum Romanum. Web. 5 May 2010.
▸ For a specific item within this database:
Caesar, Gaius Julius. *Commentarii de bello civili*. Ed. A. G. Peskett. London: W. Heinemann, 1914. Loeb Classical Library. *Corpus Scriptorum Latinorum*. Web. 5 May 2010.

In-text

(IMDb)
(*Corpus Scriptorum Latinorum*)
(Caesar) or (Caesar, *Commentarii de bello civili*)

Website, entire	Works Cited	*Digital History.* Ed. Steven Mintz. U of Houston. Web. 5 May 2010.
		Internet Public Library (IPL). School of Information, U of Michigan. Web. 5 May 2010.
	In-text	(*Digital History*)
		(*Internet Public Library*) or (IPL)
Web page, with author	Works Cited	Lipson, Charles. "Advice on Getting a Great Recommendation." *Charles Lipson.* 2010. Web. 5 May 2010.
	In-text	(Lipson) or (Lipson, "Advice")
		▸ Web pages and other online documents may not have pages. You may, however, be able to cite to a specific section (Lipson, sec. 7) or paragraph (Lipson, pars. 3–5).
Web page, no author	Works Cited	"*I Love Lucy*: Series Summary." *Sitcoms Online.* Sitcoms Online, n.d. Web. 5 May 2010.
	In-text	("*I Love Lucy*") or ("*I Love Lucy*: Series Summary")
Blog, entry or comment	Works Cited	Drezner, Daniel W. "A Dangerous Moment of Foreign Policy Fatigue." *Daniel W. Drezner.* Foreign Policy/Washingtonpost.Newsweek Interactive, 29 Oct. 2009. Web. 5 May 2010.
		▸ The MLA includes only brief coverage for these types of citations in its *Handbook for Writers of Research Papers,* 7th edition. You may need to improvise. If you want to add "Blog post" (no quotation marks) after the title of the post, go ahead. If the post has no title, this description takes its place.
		Adler, Jonathan. "The Roberts Court's Hidden ' Heart of Darkness.'" *The Volokh Conspiracy.* N.p., 28 Sept. 2009. Web. 5 May 2010.
		▸ The blog entry was made on 28 Sept. 2009. It was accessed on 5 May 2010. "N.p." means "no publisher."

Bader, Hans. Comment, 28 Sept. 2009, 12:14
p.m, on Jonathan Adler, "The Roberts
Court's Hidden 'Heart of Darkness.'" *The
Volokh Conspiracy*. N.p., 28 Sept. 2009.
Web. 5 May 2010.

▸ Bader's comment had no title and is one of
several he posted to this group blog on the same
day. Listing the time identifies it.

In-text

(Drezner) or (Drezner, "Foreign Policy Fatigue")
(Adler) or (Adler, "Roberts Court")
(Bader) or (Bader, untitled comment) or (Bader,
untitled comment, 28 Sept. 2009, 12:14 p.m.)

Video clip,
news video

Works Cited

Duck and Cover. Archer Productions/Federal
Civil Defense Administration. 1951.
Wikipedia. Web. 5 May 2010.

▸ This 1951 film was posted online in 2006 and
accessed on May 5, 2010. You can add the file type
if you want (in this case, "Ogg"—the name of a
popular format for streaming multimedia files):
Duck and Cover. Archer Productions/Federal
Civil Defense Administration. 1951.
Wikipedia. Web. 5 May 2010. Ogg file.

"Girl, 9, Drives into Cop Car." *CNN*. Cable News
Network, 24 June 2009. Posted 21 Aug.
2009. Web. 5 May 2010.

▸ Why is *Duck and Cover* in italics, but "Girl, 9,
Drives into Cop Car" placed in quotation marks?
Because MLA italicizes films and TV series, but
"quotes" individual episodes. The emergence of
new media blurs this once-bright line. In this case,
Duck and Cover is italicized because it was pro-
duced as a stand-alone film, albeit a brief one. The
footage of the girl driving into the police car on the
other hand, is a segment from one day's newscast.

In-text

(*Duck and Cover*)
("Girl, 9")

Video blog
(vlog) entry
or comment

Works Cited

Garfield, Steve. "Vlog Soup 23." *Steve
Garfield's Video Blog*. N.p., 29 Jan. 2007.
Web. 5 May 2010.

Zaidi, Ahmer. "Setting a LAMP Test Environment in Ubuntu Linux." Video tutorial. *Zipke*. N.p., 30 Aug. 2009. Web. 5 May 2010.

Jatin. Comment, 6 Oct. 2009, on Ahmer Zaidi, "Setting a LAMP Test Environment in Ubuntu Linux." *Zipke*. N.p., 30 Aug. 2009. Web. 5 May 2010.

	In-text	(Garfield) (Zaidi) (Jatin)

Podcast or video podcast (vodcast)	Works Cited	*Pseudopod: The Sound of Horror.* N.p. Web. 5 May 2010. Steinmetz, Ferrett. "Suicide Notes, Written by an Alien Mind." Podcast. Read by Phil Rossi. *Pseudopod: The Sound of Horror.* N.p., 2 Oct. 2009. Web. 5 May 2010. ▶ The Steinmetz episode was posted on October 2, 2009, and accessed on May 5, 2010. "2057: Human Civilization." Video podcast. *Discovery Channel.* Discovery Communications, 27 Dec. 2006. Web. 5 May 2010. ▶ Or Kaku, Micheo, host. "2057: Human Civilization." Video podcast. *Discovery Channel.* Discovery Communications, 27 Dec. 2006. Web. 5 May 2010.
	In-text	(*Pseudopod*) (Steinmetz) or (Steinmetz, "Suicide Notes") ("2057: Human Civilization") or (Kaku) or (Kaku, "2057")

Social networking site (Facebook, MySpace, Twitter)	Works Cited	Fawlty, Basil. Profile. *MySpace.* Web. 5 May 2010. <http://www.myspace.com/basil_fawlty>. ▶ Lest your readers find the wrong Basil Fawlty, you'd better include a URL. The same goes for all social networking sites, which are sort of like phone books with no city limits. Obama, Barack. "Info." *Facebook.* Web. 5 May 2010. <http://www.facebook.com/barackobama>.

▶ As long as you include a URL, you might as well leave out the sponsoring organization—and avoid having to write "Facebook" three times in one citation.

Obama, Barack. Comment, 20 Oct. 2009, 11:31 a.m. *Facebook*. Web. 5 May 2010. <http://www.facebook.com/barackobama>.

O'Neal, Shaquille. Comment, 20 Oct. 2009, 1:22 p.m. *Twitter*. Web. 5 May 2010. <http://twitter.com/THE_REAL_SHAQ>.

	In-text	(Fawlty profile) (Obama) or (Obama, "Info") (O'Neal) or (O'Neal, *Twitter* comment)

| E-mail and text messages, instant messages (chat), and electronic mailing lists or discussion groups | Works Cited | Leis, Kathy. "Re: New Orleans family." Message to Karen Turkish. 3 Mar. 2008. E-mail.
Mandelbaum, Michael. Message to the author. 7 Feb. 2010. E-mail.
Quigley, Mark. "National Council on Disability Calls for Health Care Reform for People with Disabilities." Message to National Council on Disability News List (NCD-NEWS-L). 30 Sept. 2009. E-mail. <http://listserv.access.gpo.gov/>.
▶ Include the URL if the mass e-mailing has been archived.
Lipson, Michael. Instant message to Jonathan Lipson. 9 Feb. 2010.
▶ Include the time for instant messages or e-mails if they are pertinent. For example: 9 Feb. 2010, 3:15 p.m. |
| | In-text | (Leis)
(Mandelbaum)
(Quigley)
(Lipson) or (Lipson, M.) |

MLA uses abbreviations frequently in Works Cited. All months are shortened, for instance, except May, June, and July. Likewise, MLA abbreviates most geographic names, such as Eur., Neth., Mex., and So. Amer. Here are some other examples:

MLA: COMMON ABBREVIATIONS IN WORKS CITED

and others	et al.	figure	fig.	paragraph	par.
appendix	app.	library	lib.	part	pt.
book	bk.	note	n	pseudonym	pseud.
chapter	ch. or chap.	notes	nn	translator	trans.
compare	cf.	number	no.	verse	v.
document	doc.	opus	op.	verses	vv.
edition	ed.	opuses	opp.	versus	vs.
editor	ed.	page	p.	volume	vol.
especially	esp.	pages	pp.		

Note: All abbreviations are lowercase, usually followed by a period. Most form their plurals by adding "s." The exceptions are note (n → nn), opus (op. → opp.), page (p. → pp.), and translator (same abbreviation).

 In citing poetry, do not use abbreviations for "line" or "lines" since a lowercase "l" is easily confused with the number one. Use either the full word or, if the meaning is clear, simply the number.

MLA: COMMON ABBREVIATIONS FOR PUBLISHERS

Alfred A. Knopf	Knopf
Basic Books	Basic
Cambridge University Press	Cambridge UP
Charles Scribner's Sons	Scribner's
Columbia University Press	Columbia UP
Cornell University Press	Cornell UP
D. C. Heath	Heath
Duke University Press	Duke UP
E. P. Dutton	Dutton
Farrar, Straus and Giroux	Farrar
HarperCollins	Harper
Harvard University Press	Harvard UP
Houghton Mifflin	Houghton
John Wiley and Sons	Wiley
Little, Brown	Little
McGraw-Hill	McGraw
MIT Press	MIT P
Oxford University Press	Oxford UP
Princeton University Press	Princeton UP
Random House	Random
Simon and Schuster	Simon

University of Chicago Press	U of Chicago P
University of Toronto Press	U of Toronto P
University Publications of America	U Publications of Am.
W. W. Norton	Norton
Yale University Press	Yale UP

MLA also eliminates the state for each publisher:

Full name: Hoboken, NJ: John Wiley and Sons, 2008.
MLA format: Hoboken: Wiley, 2008.

Despite all these abbreviations, MLA does not shorten the city where most publishers are headquartered:

Full name: New York: Routledge, 2008.
MLA format: New York: Routledge, 2008.

FAQS ABOUT MLA CITATIONS

How do I handle the citation when one author quotes another?
That happens frequently, as in Donald Kagan's book *The Peloponnesian War,* which often quotes Thucydides. Using MLA style, you might write:

Kagan approvingly quotes Thucydides, who says that Athens acquired this vital site "because of the hatred they already felt toward the Spartans" (qtd. in Kagan 14).

In your Works Cited, you include Kagan but *not* Thucydides for this particular quote. You would include the ancient Greek historian in Works Cited only if you quoted him directly elsewhere in your paper.

5 APA CITATIONS FOR THE SOCIAL SCIENCES, EDUCATION, AND BUSINESS

APA citations are widely used in psychology, education, business, and the social sciences. (Some engineering students are also required to use APA, but most use IEEE or ACSE, which are discussed in chapter 11.) Like MLA citations, APA citations are in-text. They use notes only for analysis and commentary, not to cite references. Unlike MLA, however, APA emphasizes the year of publication, which comes immediately after the author's name. That's probably because as scholarship cumulates in the sciences and empirical social sciences (where APA is used), it is important to know whether the research was conducted recently and whether it came before or after other research. At least that's the rationale.

Detailed information on the APA system is available in

- *Publication Manual of the American Psychological Association,* 6th ed. (Washington, DC: American Psychological Association, 2010).

Like *The Chicago Manual of Style* and MLA style books, the APA manual should be available in your library's reference section.

To get started, let's look at APA references for a journal article, a chapter in an edited book, and a book as they appear at the end of a paper. APA calls this a "Reference List." (MLA calls it "Works Cited," and Chicago calls it a "Bibliography.")

Lipson, C. (1991). Why are some international agreements informal? *International Organization, 45,* 495–538.
Lipson, C. (1994). Is the future of collective security like the past? In G. Downs (Ed.), *Collective security beyond the cold war* (pp. 105–131). Ann Arbor: University of Michigan Press.
Lipson, C. (2003). *Reliable partners: How democracies have made a separate peace.* Princeton, NJ: Princeton University Press.

This list for the distinguished author C. Lipson follows another APA rule. All entries for a single author are arranged by year of publication, beginning with the earliest. If there were two entries for a particular year, say 2011, they would be alphabetized by title and the first would be labeled (2011a), the second (2011b). A future publication would be cited as "(in press)." Also note the APA's rules for capitalizing book and article titles. They are treated like sentences, with only the first words capitalized. If there's a colon in the title, the first word after the colon is also capitalized. Proper nouns are capitalized, of course, just as they are in sentences.

In these reference lists, single-author entries precede those with co-authors. So Pinker, S. (as a sole author) would precede Pinker, S., & Jones, B. In the APA system, multiple authors are joined by an ampersand "&" rather than the word "and." It is not clear why. Just accept it as a rule, like how many minutes are in a soccer game.

The authors' first names are always reduced to initials. That makes it different from MLA and Chicago, as does its frequent use of commas and parentheses.

When works are cited in the text, the citation includes the author's name, for example (Wilson, 2011d), unless the author's name has already been mentioned in that sentence. If the sentence includes the author's name, the citation omits it. For instance: Nye (2011) presents considerable data to back up his claims. If you include a direct quote, then you *must* include the page number in the citation. For instance: "The policy is poorly conceived," according to Nye (2011, p. 12).

The examples in this chapter focus on psychology, education, other social sciences, and business, where APA citations are most widely used, just as the MLA examples focus on the humanities, where that style is common.

To make it easy to find the APA citations you need, I've listed them here alphabetically, along with the pages where they are described.

INDEX OF APA CITATIONS IN THIS CHAPTER

APA: REFERENCE LIST AND IN-TEXT CITATIONS

| Book, one author | Reference list | Devlin, L. (2007). *Chief of station, Congo: Fighting the Cold War in a hot zone.* New York, NY: Public Affairs. |

▸ APA requires the state even for well-known cities. Exception: if the name of a university publisher includes the state, you can omit it (e.g., Ann Arbor: University of Michigan Press).

Naughton, B. (2007). *The Chinese economy: Transitions and growth.* Cambridge, MA: MIT Press.

Macdonald, D. (2007). *Business and environmental politics in Canada.* Peterborough, Ontario, Canada: Broadview Press.

▸ Although U.S. states are abbreviated, Canadian provinces and territories are spelled out and the country name is included.

In-text

(Devlin, 2007)
(Naughton, 2007)
(Macdonald, 2007)

Books and articles, several by same author	Reference list	Posner, R. C. (2007a). *Countering terrorism.* Lanham, MD: Rowman & Littlefield with the Hoover Institution. Posner, R. C. (2007b). *Economic analysis of law* (7th ed.). New York, NY: Aspen Law and Business. Posner, R. C. (2007c). *The little book of plagiarism.* New York, NY: Pantheon. Posner, R. C. (2006a). *Not a suicide pact: The Constitution in a time of national emergency.* New York, NY: Oxford University Press. Posner, R. C. (2006b). *Uncertain shield: The U.S. intelligence system in the throes of reform.* Lanham, MD: Rowman & Littlefield with the Hoover Institution. Posner R. C., & Becker, G. S. (2006). *Suicide and risk-taking: An economic approach.* Unpublished paper, University of Chicago. ▸ Note that the author's name is repeated. APA does not use dashes for repetition. ▸ When the same author or coauthors have several publications in the same year, list them alphabetically (by the first significant word in the title). Label them as "a," "b," and "c." The last 2006 item by Posner is *not* labeled "c" because its authorship is different. ▸ Coauthored books like Posner & Becker follow a writer's single-author ones, in the alphabetical order of the second author's name.
	In-text	(Posner, 2007a, 2007b, 2007c, 2006a, 2006b; Posner & Becker, 2006)
Book, multiple authors	Reference list	Fubini, D., Price, C., & Zollo, M. (2007). *Mergers: Leadership, performance and corporate health.* New York, NY: Palgrave Macmillan. Wells, L. T., & Ahmed, R. (2007). *Making foreign investment safe: Property rights and national sovereignty.* New York, NY: Oxford University Press.

Butcher, T., Guo., X., Harris, J., Lette, K., Mankell, H., Moggach, D., . . . Welsh, I. (2010). *Because I'm a girl*. New York, NY: Random House.

► Name up to seven authors; for eight or more, list the first six followed by an ellipsis (three spaced periods) and then the name of the last author.

In-text

(Fubini, Price, & Zollo, 2007)
(Wells & Ahmed, 2007)

► For two authors, always list both. For three to five authors, name all authors in the first citation. Beginning with the second reference, name only the first author, then add "et al.": (Fubini et al., 2007)
► For six or more authors, name only the first author, then add "et al." for all citations.
► Use "&" within parenthetical references but not in the text itself.

Book, multiple editions

Reference list

Schweitzer, S. O. (2007). *Pharmaceutical economics and policy* (2nd ed.). New York, NY: Oxford University Press.

► If it says "revised edition" rather than "2nd edition," use "(Rev. ed.)" in the same spot.

Strunk, W., Jr., & White, E. B. (2009). *The elements of style* (50th anniversary ed.). New York, NY: Longman.

In-text

(Strunk & White, 2009)

► To refer to a specific page for a quotation:

(Strunk & White, 2009, p. 12)

Book, corporate author or no author

Reference list

University of Michigan, Office of Student Publications. (2007). *2007 alumni directory*. Bloomington, IN: University Publishing Corporation.

American Psychological Association. (2010). *Publication manual of the American Psychological Association* (6th ed.). Washington, DC: Author.

> If the publisher is the same as the author, write "Author" in place of the former.

The bluebook: A uniform system of citation (18th ed.). (2005). Cambridge, MA: Harvard Law Review Association.

> For multiple editions without authors, the form is *Title* (edition). (year). City, STATE: Publisher.

In-text	(University of Michigan, 2007)

> Abbreviate a corporate author on subsequent mentions only, and only if the abbreviation will be immediately recognizable to readers.

(American Psychological Association [APA], 2010)

> Subsequent references are (APA, 2010).

(*Bluebook*, 2005)

Book, edited — Reference list

Bakker, K. (Ed.). (2007). *Eau Canada: The future of Canada's water*. Vancouver, British Columbia, Canada: University of British Columbia Press.

Bosworth, M., & Flavin, J. (Eds.). (2007). *Race, gender, and punishment: From colonialism to the war on terror*. New Brunswick, NJ: Rutgers University Press.

Aikhenvald, A. Y., & Dixon, R. M. W. (Eds.). (2007). *Grammars in contact: A cross-linguistic typology*. Oxford, England: Oxford University Press.

In-text

(Bakker, 2007)
(Bosworth & Flavin, 2007)
(Aikhenvald & Dixon, 2007)

Book, online and e-books — Reference list

Reed, J. (1922). *Ten days that shook the world* [Etext 3076]. Retrieved from http://www.gutenberg.org/dirs/etext02/10daz10.txt

> APA does *not* put a period after the URL, making it different from most other reference styles.

> And APA does *not* want access dates—except for sources that may change over time (think *Wikipedia* article).

Toy, E. C., & Klamen, D. (2009). *Case files: Psychiatry* (3rd ed.) [Kindle version]. Retrieved from http://www.amazon.com/

▸ Electronic retrieval information takes the place of the publisher location and name. That's code for URL. If the URL is very long, cite the home page (as in the Toy and Klamen example).

▸ APA says to put important but "nonroutine" information in square brackets following the title (and after any parenthetical information— about edition, volumes, etc.). That's where you put the e-book version.

	In-text	(Reed, 1922) (Toy & Klamen, 2009)
Multivolume work	Reference list	Johansen, B. E. (2006). *Global warming in the 21st century* (Vols. 1–3). Westport, CT: Praeger. Pflanze, O. (1963–1990). *Bismarck and the development of Germany* (Vols. 1–3). Princeton, NJ: Princeton University Press.
	In-text	(Johansen, 2006) (Pflanze, 1963–1990)
Single volume in a multivolume work	Reference list	Johansen, B. E. (2006). *Global warming in the 21st century: Vol. 1. Our evolving climate crisis.* Westport, CT: Praeger. Pflanze, O. (1990). *Bismarck and the development of Germany: Vol. 3. The period of fortification, 1880–1898.* Princeton, NJ: Princeton University Press.
	In-text	(Johansen, 2006) (Pflanze, 1990)
Reprint of earlier edition	Reference list	Smith, A. (1976). *An inquiry into the nature and causes of the wealth of nations.* E. Cannan (Ed.). Chicago, IL: University of Chicago Press. (Original work published 1776) ▸ There is no period after the parenthesis.

	In-text	(Smith, 1776/1976)
Translated volume	Reference list	Weber, M. (1958). *The Protestant ethic and the spirit of capitalism*. T. Parsons (Trans.). New York, NY: Charles Scribner's Sons. (Original work published 1904–1905)
	In-text	(Weber, 1904–1905/1958)
Foreign language volume	Reference list	Weber, M. (2005). *Die protestantische ethik und der Geist des Kapitalismus* [The Protestant ethic and the spirit of capitalism]. Erftstadt, Germany: Area Verlag. (Original work published 1904–1905)
	In-text	(Weber, 1904–1905/2005)
Chapter in edited book	Reference list	Cohen, B. J. (2006). The macrofoundations of monetary power. In D. M. Andrews (Ed.), *International monetary power* (pp. 31–50). Ithaca, NY: Cornell University Press. ► Chapter titles are not in quotes or italics.
	In-text	(Cohen, 2006)
Journal article, one author	Reference list	Meirowitz, A. (2007). Communication and bargaining in the spatial model. *International Journal of Game Theory, 35*, 251–266. doi:10.1007/s00182-006-0052-3 ► Article titles are not in quotes or italics. ► The journal's volume number is italicized, but the issue number and pages are not. The word "volume" (or "vol.") is omitted. ► There's no need to name a specific issue if the journal pages are numbered continuously throughout the year. However, if each issue begins with page 1, then the issue's number or month is necessary to find the article: *45*(2), 15–30.

> ▸ The string of numbers at the end of the citation is called a Digital Object Identifier (DOI). Most scholarly journal articles assign them, and APA wants you to include a DOI for every journal article that has one—even if you're citing print. A DOI is a permanent ID and preferable to a URL. You'll generally find it on the first page of an article. Readers can paste the DOI into a DOI resolver (available from CrossRef.org,), which will direct them to at least an abstract of the article—wherever it is posted. If you're citing an article online and don't see a DOI, list a URL instead.

	In-text	(Meirowitz, 2007)

Journal article, multiple authors	Reference list	Koremenos, B., Lipson, C., & Snidal, D. (2001). The rational design of international institutions. *International Organization*, *55*, 761–799. doi:10.1162/002081801317193592 Guo, S., Chen, D., Zhou, D., Sun, H., Wu, G., Haile, C., . . . Zhang, X. (2007). Association of functional catechol O-methyl transferase (COMT) Val108Met polymorphism with smoking severity and age of smoking initiation in Chinese male smokers. *Psychopharmacology*, *190*, 449–456. doi:10.1007/s00213-006-0628-4 ▸ Name up to seven authors; for eight or more, list the first six followed by an ellipsis and then the last author's name.
	In-text	(Koremenos, Lipson, & Snidal, 2001) for first reference. (Koremenos et al., 2001) for second reference and after. ▸ When a work has three to five authors, name all of them in the first textual reference. After that, use only the first author's name plus "et al." (Guo et al., 2007)

► When a work has six authors or more, name only the first one plus "et al." For example, this would be the first mention of the Guo article:

In their study of Chinese male smokers, Guo et al. (2007) find an association . . .

Journal article, online	Reference list	Kane, D., & Park, J. M. (2009). The puzzle of Korean Christianity: Geopolitical networks and religious conversion in early twentieth-century East Asia. *American Journal of Sociology, 115*, 365–404. doi:10.1086/599246

► Always list a DOI if there is one (even for print).

Baggetun, R., & Wasson, B. (2006). Self-regulated learning and open writing. *European Journal of Education 41*, 453–472. doi:10.1111/j.1465-3435 .2006.00276.x

Mitchell, T. (2002). McJihad: Islam in the U.S. global order. *Social Text, 20*(4), 1–18. doi:10.1215/01642472-20-4_73-1

► The issue number (4, in parentheses but not in italics) is included because each issue of this journal starts over at page 1.
► If you don't see a DOI, list the URL of the journal's home page or—if you get the article from a database—the URL of that. If the full URL is relatively short, you can include the whole thing.

Clark, M., Isaacks-Downton, G., Redlin-Frazier, S., & Wells, N. (2006). Use of preferred music to reduce emotional distress and symptom activity during radiation therapy. *Journal of Music Therapy 43*(3), 247–265. Retrieved from http://www.ncbi.nlm.nih .gov/pubmed/17037953

In-text

(Kane & Park, 2009)
(Baggetun & Wasson, 2006)
(Mitchell, 2002)
(Clark, Isaacks-Downton, Redlin-Frazier & Wells, 2006) then (Clark et al., 2006)

Journal article, foreign language	Reference list	Maignan, I., & Swaen, V. (2004). La responsabilité sociale d'une organisation: Intégration des perspectives marketing et managériale. *Revue Française du Marketing, 200,* 51–66. ▸ Or Maignan, I., & Swaen, V. (2004). La responsabilité sociale d'une organisation: Intégration des perspectives marketing et managériale [The social responsibility of an organization: Integration of marketing and managerial perspectives]. *Revue Française du Marketing, 200,* 51–66.
	In-text	(Maignan & Swaen, 2004)
Newspaper or magazine article, no author	Reference list	State senator's indictment details demands on staff. (2007, February 11). *The New York Times* (National ed.), p. 23. ▸ APA includes an initial *The* in newspaper and magazine titles. ▸ Newspaper page numbers include "p." or "pp." America and China talk climate change: Heating up or cooling down? (2009, June 11). *The Economist 391*(8635), 61. ▸ APA treats magazines much like journals. If you can't determine the volume and issue numbers, leave them out and put "p." or "pp." before the page number(s).
	In-text	("State senator's indictment," 2007) ("Climate change," 2009)
Newspaper or magazine article, with author	Reference list	Martin, A., & Morgenson, G. (2009, October 31). Can Citigroup carry its own weight? *The New York Times* (New York ed.), p. BU1. ▸ If an article appears on nonconsecutive pages, give all numbers, separated by commas: e.g., pp. BU1, BU5–BU6, BU9.

	In-text	(Martin & Morgenson, 2009) or, if necessary, (Martin & Morgenson, 2009, October 31)
Newspaper or magazine article, online	Reference list	Wilson, S. (2009, November 2). Karzai win complicates White House strategy for Afghanistan. *The Washington Post*. Retrieved from http://www.washingtonpost.com/ Pandey, S. (2007, February 11). I read the news today, oh boy. *The Los Angeles Times* (Home ed.), p. M6. Retrieved from http://www.proquest.com/
	In-text	(Wilson, 2009) or (Wilson, 2009, November 2) (Pandey, 2007) or (Pandey, 2007, February 11)
Review	Reference list	Lane, J. H. (2006, December). [Review of the book *A kinder, gentler America: Melancholia and the mythical 1950s*, by M. Caputi]. *Perspectives on Politics, 4*, 749–750. Ferguson, N. (2007, February 4). Ameliorate, contain, coerce, destroy [Review of the book *The utility of force: The art of war in the modern world*, by R. Smith]. *New York Times Book Review*, 14–15.
	In-text	(Lane, 2006) (Ferguson, 2007)
Unpublished paper, poster session, dissertation, or thesis	Reference list	Leeds, A. (2007, February). *Interests, institutions, and foreign policy consistency*. Paper presented at the Program on International Politics, Economics, and Security, University of Chicago. ▸ Only the month and year are needed for papers. Tomz, M., & Van Houweling, R. P. (2009, August). *Candidate inconsistency and voter choice*. Unpublished manuscript, Stanford University and University of California, Berkeley. Retrieved from http://www.stanford.edu/~tomz/working/TomzVanHouweling-2009–08.pdf

    ► Other categories include "Manuscript submitted for publication" and "Manuscript in preparation."

Noble, L. (2006). *One goal, multiple strategies: Engagement in Sino-American WTO accession negotiations.* Unpublished master's thesis, University of British Columbia, Vancouver, Canada.

    ► APA considers any thesis or dissertation that's not available from a commercial database to be unpublished.

Sullivan, S. P. (2004). *Education through sport: Athletics in American Indian boarding schools of New Mexico, 1885–1940* (Doctoral dissertation, University of New Mexico). Retrieved from ProQuest Dissertations and Theses (AAT 3154951).

    ► That parenthetical string of letters and numbers at the end is the accession number—helpful in finding the item in the database.

    ► APA doesn't require the name of the institution for a thesis or dissertation retrieved from a commercial database, but why not add it anyway?

In-text

(Leeds, 2007)
(Tomz & Van Houweling, 2009)
(Noble, 2006)
(Sullivan, 2004)

Preprint   Reference list   Allesina, S. (2009, November 2). *Accelerating the pace of discovery by changing the peer review algorithm* [Preprint]. Retrieved from http://lanl.arxiv.org/PS_cache/arxiv/pdf/0911/0911.0344v1.pdf

    ► arXiv is a collection facility for scientific "e-prints." Some of them have been published and some have not. APA recommends updating your references when you're close to finishing your paper; if you've cited a preprint that's since been published, cite the published journal article.

▸ Some journals publish articles online ahead of time. You can cite these in one of two ways (and again, update the reference when the article gets published):

Ravigné, V., Dieckmann, U., & Olivieri, I. (2009). Live where you thrive: Joint evolution of habitat choice and local adaptation facilitates specialization and promotes diversity. *The American Naturalist*. Advance online publication. doi:10.1086/605369

▸ Or

Ravigné, V., Dieckmann, U., & Olivieri, I. (in press). Live where you thrive: Joint evolution of habitat choice and local adaptation facilitates specialization and promotes diversity. *The American Naturalist, 174*, E141–E169. doi:10.1086/605369

In-text

(Allesina, 2009)
(Ravigné, Dieckmann, & Olivieri, 2009) or (Ravigné, Dieckmann, & Olivieri, in press)
▸ Subsequent references are (Ravigné et al., 2009) or (Ravigné et al., in press)

Abstract   **Reference list**

Barahona, C., & Levy, S. (2007). The best of both worlds: Producing national statistics using participatory methods [Abstract]. *World Development, 35*, 326. doi:10.1016/j.worlddev.2006.10.006
▸ Abstract obtained from original source. Use the same format to cite abstracts from published conference proceedings. And remember that APA wants you to include a DOI for any source that has one—printed or online. If you cite an online source with no DOI, include a URL.

Hatchard, J. (2006). Combating transnational crime in Africa: Problems and perspectives. *Journal of African Law, 50*, 145–160. Abstract obtained from *African Studies Abstracts Online, 17*, Abstract No. 21 (2007). Retrieved from http://hdl.handle.net/1887/11948
▸ Abstract obtained from secondary source.

	In-text	(Barahona & Levy, 2007) (Hatchard, 2006/2007) ▶ If the secondary abstract source is published in a different year from the primary source, cite both dates, separated by a slash.
Microfilm, microfiche	Reference list	U.S. House of Representatives. Records. Southern Claims Commission. (1871–1880). *First report (1871)*. Washington, DC: National Archives Microfilm Publication, P2257, Frames 0145–0165. Conservative Party (UK). (1919). *Annual report of the executive committee to central council, March 11–November 18, 1919*. Archive of the British Conservative Party, Microfiche card 143. Woodbridge, CT: Gale/ Primary Source Microfilm, 1998. (Original material located in Conservative Party Archive, Bodleian Library, Oxford, England.) ▶ You do not need to include the location of the original material, but you are welcome to.
	In-text	(U.S. House, 1871–1880) (Conservative Party, 1919)
Encyclopedia, hard copy and online	Reference list	Balkans: History. (1987). In *Encyclopaedia Britannica* (15th ed., Vol. 14, pp. 570–588). Chicago, IL: Encyclopaedia Britannica. Balkans. (2009). *Encyclopaedia Britannica online*. Retrieved from http://www .britannica.com/EBchecked/topic /50325/Balkans Graham, G. (2007). Behaviorism. In E. N. Zalta (Ed.), *The Stanford encyclopedia of philosophy*. Retrieved from http://plato .stanford.edu/entries/behaviorism/ Emotion. (n.d.). *Wikipedia*. Retrieved May 5, 2010, from http://en.wikipedia.org/wiki /Emotion ▶ Though APA does not recommend access dates for most types of sources, they do recommend them for undated sources that are subject to frequent updates—like this *Wikipedia* article.

	In-text	(Balkans: History, 1987)
		▸ You may wish to include the subtitle, "history," in this case to help the reader if the main article is long or if you are citing several articles with similar titles and dates.
		(Balkans, 2009)
		(Graham, 2007)
		(Emotion, n.d.)

Reference book, hard copy and online	Reference list	Pendergast, S., & Pendergast, T. (Eds.). (2003). *Reference guide to world literature* (3rd ed., 2 vols.). Detroit, MI: St. James Press.
		Pendergast, S., & Pendergast, T. (Eds.). (2003). *Reference guide to world literature* [eBook version]. Retrieved from http://www.gale.cengage.com/
		Colman, A. M. (2001). *A dictionary of psychology*. Retrieved from http://www.oxfordreference.com
		Woods, T. (2003). The social contract (du contrat social), prose by Jean-Jacques Rousseau, 1762. In Pendergast, S., & Pendergast, T. (Eds.), *Reference guide to world literature* (3rd ed., Vol. 2, pp. 1512–1513). Detroit, MI: St. James Press.
		Obama marks Holocaust in Germany, D-Day in France; visits WWII sites in Buchenwald, Normandy. (2009, June 11). Retrieved from http://www.2facts.com/article/2009492010
		▸ Or
		Obama marks Holocaust in Germany, D-Day in France; visits WWII sites in Buchenwald, Normandy. (2009, June 11). Retrieved from *Facts On File World News Digest* database. (Accession No. 2009492010)
	In-text	(Pendergast & Pendergast, 2003)
		(Colman, 2001)
		(Woods, 2003)
		("Obama marks Holocaust," 2009)
		▸ Quotation marks are used for an article title that is cited in-text.

Dictionary, hard copy, online, and CD-ROM	Reference list	Gerrymander. (2003). *Merriam-Webster's collegiate dictionary* (11th ed.). Springfield, MA: Merriam-Webster. Protest, *v.* (1971). *Compact edition of the Oxford English dictionary* (Vol. 2, p. 2335). Oxford, England: Oxford University Press. ▸ The word "protest" is both a noun and a verb. Here, I am citing the verb. Class, *n.* (n.d.). *Dictionary.com unabridged.* Retrieved May 5, 2010, from http:// dictionary.reference.com/browse/class Anxious. (2000). *American heritage dictionary of the English language* (4th ed.) [CD-ROM version]. Boston, MA: Houghton Mifflin.
	In-text	("Protest," 1971)

Bible, Qur'an (Koran)	Reference list	▸ Not needed, except to reference a particular version. *The five books of Moses: A translation with commentary.* (2004). Robert Alter (Trans. & Ed.). New York, NY: Norton.
	In-text	Deut. 1:2 (New Revised Standard Version). ▸ List the version you are using the first time it is mentioned in the text. After that, you omit the version. Gen. 1:1, 1:3–5, 2:4. ▸ Books of the Bible can be abbreviated, such as Exod., Lev., Num., Cor., and so on. Qur'an 18:65–82.

Classical works	Reference list	▸ Not needed, except to reference a particular version. Plato. (2006). *The republic.* R. E. Allen (Trans.). New Haven, CT: Yale University Press. (Original work, approximately 360 BC) Virgil. (2006). *The Aeneid.* R. Fagles (Trans.). New York, NY: Viking, 2006. (Original work, approximately 19–29 BC)

| | In-text | (Plato, trans. 2006) |
| | | (Virgil, trans. 2006) |

Speech, academic talk, or course lecture	Reference list	Collins, P. H. (2009, August 9). Presidential address at the annual meeting of the American Sociological Association, San Francisco, CA.
		Rector, N. (2007, March 6). Course lecture at the University of Toronto, Toronto, Ontario, Canada.
	In-text	(Collins, 2009)
		(Rector, 2007)

Personal communication or interview	Reference list	Atwood, M. (2008, October 13). Atwood on debt: Kenneth Whyte talks to Margaret Atwood about her new book and debt's dark side [Interview]. *Maclean's, 121*(40), 96–97.
		Smith, H. (1941). Interview by J. H. Faulk [Audio file]. Library of Congress, Archive of Folk Culture, American Folklife Center, Washington, D.C. Retrived from http://hdl.loc.gov/loc.afc/afc9999001.5499a
	In-text	(Atwood, 2008)
		(Smith, 1941)
		(J. M. Coetzee, personal interview, May 5, 2010)
		(D. A. Grossberg, personal communication, May 5, 2010)
		(anonymous U.S. Marine, recently returned from Afghanistan, interviewed by author, May 5, 2010)

▸ The reference list includes published or archived interviews, like Atwood's and Smith's, but not personal communications such as private conversation, faxes, letters, or interviews that cannot be accessed by other investigators. Therefore, in-text citations for personal communications—like the ones for Coetzee, Grossberg, and the anonymous U.S. Marine—should fully describe the item, including the full date.

Television program	Reference list	Long, T. (Writer), & Moore, S. D. (Director). (2002). Bart vs. Lisa vs. 3rd grade [Television series episode]. In B. Oakley & J. Weinstein (Producers), *The Simpsons*. Fox. Carlock, R. (Writer), & Miller, M. B. (Director). (2009). Into the crevasse [Television series episode]. In T. Fey, L. Michaels, M. Klein, D. Miner, & R. Carlock (Producers), *30 Rock*. NBC. Retrieved from http://www.hulu.com/30-rock
	In-text	(Long & Moore, 2002) (Carlock & Miller, 2009)
Film	Reference list	Wallis, H. B. (Producer), & Huston, J. (Director/Writer). (1941). *The Maltese falcon* [Motion picture]. H. Bogart, M. Astor, P. Lorre, S. Greenstreet, E. Cook Jr. (Performers). Based on novel by D. Hammett. Warner Studios. United States: Warner Home Video, DVD. (2000) ▸ Required: You must include the title, director, studio, and year released. ▸ Optional: the actors, producers, screenwriters, editors, cinematographers, and other information. Include what you need for analysis in your paper, in order of importance to your analysis. Their names appear between the title and the distributor.
	In-text	(Wallis & Huston, 1941/2000)
Photograph	Reference list	Adams, A. (1927). *Monolith, the face of Half Dome, Yosemite National Park* [Photograph]. Art Institute, Chicago.
	In-text	(Adams, 1927)
Photograph, online	Reference list	Adams, A. (1927). *Monolith, the face of Half Dome, Yosemite National Park* [Photograph]. Art Institute, Chicago. Retrieved from http://www.hctc.commnet.edu/artmuseum/anseladams/details/pdf/monlith.pdf

	In-text	(Adams, 1927)

| Figures: map, chart, graph, or table | Credit or explanation for figure or table | ▸ Citation for a map, chart, graph, or table normally appears as a credit below the item rather than as an in-text citation.

Note. 2006 election results, House of Representatives map. *Washington Post.* Retrieved from http://projects.washingtonpost.com/elections/keyraces/map/

Note. From M. E. J. Newman (n.d.), Maps of the 2008 US presidential election. Retrieved from http://www-personal.umich.edu/~mejn/election/2008/

Note. Satellite map, California (2009) [Detail]. National Geographic/Microsoft. Retrieved from http://maps.nationalgeographic.com/

Note. From K. Menkhaus (2006/2007), Governance without government in Somalia: Spoilers, state building, and the politics of coping. *International Security, 31* (Winter), 79, fig. 1.

▸ Give a descriptive title to your maps, charts, graphs, and tables. With this description, the reader should understand the item without having to refer to the text.

Note. All figures are rounded to nearest percentile.

▸ This is a general note explaining information in a table.

$*p < .05$ $**p < .01$. Both are two-tailed tests.

▸ This is a probability note for a table of statistics. |
| | Reference list | 2006 election results, House of Representatives map. (2006). *Washington Post.* Retrieved from http://projects.washingtonpost.com/elections/keyraces/map/

Newman, M. E. J. (n.d.). Maps of the 2008 US presidential election. Retrieved from http://www-personal.umich.edu/~mejn/election/2008/

Satellite map, California. (2009). [Detail]. National Geographic/Microsoft. Retrieved from http://maps.nationalgeographic.com/ |

		Menkhaus, K. (2006/2007). Governance without government in Somalia: Spoilers, state building, and the politics of coping. *International Security, 31*(Winter), 74–106. doi:10.1162/isec.2007.31.3.74
	In-text	(2006 election results, House, 2006) (Newman, n.d.) (Satellite map, California, 2009) (Menkhaus, 2006/2007)
Musical recording	Reference list	Johnson, R. (1998). Last fair deal gone down. On *Robert Johnson: King of the Delta blues singers* (Exp. ed.) [CD]. Columbia/Legacy. (Originally recorded 1936) ▸ "Exp. ed." = expanded edition.
	In-text	(Johnson, 1998, track 5)
Advertise- ment, hard copy and online	Reference list	Advertisement for *Letters from Iwo Jima* [Motion picture]. (2007, February 6). *New York Times*, p. B4. Pillarless. And, for that matter, peerless. (2007, February 12). [Advertisement for Mercedes-Benz 2007 CL-class automobiles]. *New Yorker 82*(49), 26. Tab cola. [ca. late 1960s]. Be a mindsticker [Television advertisement]. Retrieved from http://www.dailymotion.com/video /x2s3qi_1960s-tab-commercial-be-a -mindstick_ads ▸ Enclose estimated dates in square brackets.
	In-text	(advertisement for *Letters from Iwo Jima*, 2007) (Pillarless, 2007) (Tab cola, [ca. late 1960s])
Government document, hard copy and online	Reference list	*A bill to promote the national security by providing for a national defense establishment: Hearings on S. 758 before the Committee on Armed Service, Senate,* 80th Cong. 1 (1947).

- "80th Cong. 1" refers to page 1 (not to the first session). If the reference was to testimony by a specific individual, that would appear after the date: (1947) (testimony of Gen. George Marshall).
- For documents printed by the Government Printing Office, give the full name rather than the initials "GPO."

U.S. Census Bureau. (2009). *Statistical abstract of the U.S.* Washington, DC: U.S. Government Printing Office.

- Or

U.S. Census Bureau. (2009). *Statistical abstract of the U.S.* Retrieved from http://www.census.gov/compendia/statab/

Public Safety Canada (2009, October 30). Final Olympic security Exercise Gold underway Monday. Retrieved from http://www.publicsafety.gc.ca/media/nr/2009/nr20091030-eng.asp

Federal Bureau of Investigation [FBI]. (1972). *Investigation of John Lennon* (248 pages). Retrieved from http://foia.fbi.gov/foiaindex/lennon.htm

In-text

(*Bill to promote national security*, 1947)
(U.S. Census Bureau, 2009)
(Public Safety Canada, 2009)
(FBI, 1972)

Software	Reference list	• Standard software is not included in the reference list.
	In-text	(Dreamweaver CS4, 2008) (iTunes 9.0.3.15, 2010) (Stata 11, 2009)
Database	Reference list	Maryland Department of Assessments and Taxation. (2009). *Real property data search* (Version 2.0). Retrieved from http://sdatcert3.resiusa.org/rp_rewrite/

U.S. Copyright Office. (2009). *Search copyright
      records*. Retrieved from http://www
      .copyright.gov/records/
Gleditsch, K. S., & Chiozza, G. (2009). *Archigos:
      A data base on leaders, 1875–2004* (Version
      2.9). Retrieved from http://mail
      .rochester.edu/%7Ehgoemans
      /data.htm
United Nations Treaty Collection. (2010).
      Databases. Retrieved from http://treaties
      .un.org/
      ▸ For a specific item within this database:
International convention for the protection of
      all persons from enforced disappearance.
      (2006). In United Nations Treaty Collection,
      Databases. Retrieved from http://treaties
      .un.org/doc/source/RecentTexts/XIX_46
      _english.pdf

In-text   (Maryland Department of Assessments, 2009)
      (U.S. Copyright Office, 2009)
      (Gleditsch & Chiozza, 2009)
      (United Nations Treaty Collection, 2010)
      ("International convention on enforced
      disappearance," 2006)

Diagnostic   Reference list   *MMPI-2: Restructured clinical (RC) scales.*
test   (2003). Minneapolis: University of
                                    Minnesota Press.
Ben-Porath, Y. S., & Tellegen, A. (2008). *MMPI-
      2-RF (Minnesota Multiphasic Personality
      Inventory-2): Manual for administration,
      scoring, and interpretation*. Minneapolis:
      University of Minnesota Press.
      ▸ Manual for administering the test.
Tellegen, A., Ben-Porath, Y. S., McNulty, J. L.,
      Arbisi, P. A., Graham, J. R., & Kaemmer, B.
      (2003). *The MMPI-2 restructured clinical
      (RC) scales: Development, validation, and
      interpretation*. Minneapolis: University of
      Minnesota Press.
      ▸ Interpretive manual for the test.

Q Local (Version 2.3) [Computer software]. (2009). Minneapolis, MN: Pearson Assessments.

▸ Scoring software for the test.

In-text

(*MMPI-2 RC scales*, 2003)
(Ben-Porath & Tellegen, 2008)
(Tellegen et al., 2003)
(Q Local, 2009)

Diagnostic manual

Reference list

Pierangelo, R., & Giuliani, G. (2007). *The educator's diagnostic manual of disabilities and disorders*. San Francisco, CA: Jossey-Bass.

American Psychiatric Association. (2000). *Diagnostic and statistical manual of mental disorders* (4th ed., text rev. [*DSM-IV-TR*]). Washington, DC: Author.

▸ Or

American Psychiatric Association. (2000). *Diagnostic and statistical manual of mental disorders* (4th ed., text rev. [*DSM-IV-TR*]). doi:10.1176/appi.books.9780890423349

In-text

(Pierangelo & Giuliani, 2007)
(American Psychiatric Association, *Diagnostic and statistical manual of mental disorders* [*DSM-IV-TR*], 2000) for the first use only. (*DSM-IV-TR*) for second use and later. Title is italicized.

Website, entire

Reference list

Digital history [Website]. (2009). S. Mintz (Ed.). Retrieved from http://www.digitalhistory.uh.edu/

IPL: The Internet public library [Website]. (2009). Retrieved from http://www.ipl.org/

Yale University, History Department [Home page]. (2010). Retrieved February 12, 2010, from http://www.yale.edu/history/

▸ If a website or web page does not show a date when it was copyrighted or updated, then list (n.d.) where the year normally appears.

	In-text	(*Digital history*, 2009)
		(*IPL*, 2009)
		(Yale History Department, 2010)

Web page, with author	Reference list	Lipson, C. (2010). "Advice on getting a great recommendation." Retrieved from http://www.charleslipson.com/courses/Getting-a-good-recommendation.htm
	In-text	(Lipson, 2010)

Web page, no author	Reference list	*The Dick Van Dyke show:* Series summary. (n.d.). *Sitcoms online.* Retrieved from http://www.sitcomsonline.com/thedickvandykeshow.html
	In-text	(*The Dick Van Dyke show:* Series summary, n.d.)

Blog, entry or comment	Reference list	Tobias, A. (2009, October 30). Sober stuff [Weblog post]. *Andrew Tobias: Money and other subjects.* Retrieved from http://www.andrewtobias.com/bkoldcolumns/091030.html

► If this entry had no title, it would be cited as:

Tobias, A. (2009, October 30). Untitled entry [Weblog post]. *Andrew Tobias: Money and . . .*

Kerr, O. (2007, February 12). Can Congress force the Supreme Court to televise proceedings? [Weblog post]. *The Volokh conspiracy.* Retrieved from http://volokh.com/

Crunchy Frog. (2007, February 12). Re: Can Congress force the Supreme Court to televise proceedings? [Weblog comment]. *The Volokh conspiracy.* Retrieved from http://volokh.com/posts/1171256603.shtml#187745

► If the wonderfully named "Crunchy Frog" had commented several times the same day and there was no link to a specific comment, then you should include the time: (2007, February 12, 12:53 a.m.).

	In-text	(Tobias, 2009)
		(Kerr, 2007)
		(Crunchy Frog, 2007)

Video clip, news video	Reference list	Archer Productions (Producer). (1951). *Duck and cover* [Video file]. Produced for the Federal Civil Defense Administration. Retrieved from http://en.wikipedia.org/wiki/File:DuckandC1951.ogg
		Girl, 9, drives into cop car [Video file]. (2009, June 24). Retrieved from http://www.cnn.com/video/#/video/us/2009/08/21/weakley.tn.child.driver.wkrn
		▸ When the URL is very long and the video can be found on a searchable site, you may choose to include only the site's main page: Retrieved from http://www.cnn.com/
	In-text	(Archer Productions, 1951)
		("Girl, 9, drives into cop car," 2009)

Video blog (vlog)	Reference list	Garfield, S. (2007, January 29). Vlog soup 23 [Video post]. *Steve Garfield's video blog.* Retrieved from http://stevegarfield.blogs.com/videoblog/2007/01/vlog_soup_23.html
		Zaidi, A. (2009, August 30). Setting a LAMP test environment in Ubuntu Linux [Video post]. Retrieved from http://zipke.com/2009/08/setting-a-lamp-test-environment-in-ubuntu-linux/
		Jatin. (2009, October 6). Re: Setting a LAMP test environment in Ubuntu Linux [Comment on video post]. Retrieved from http://zipke.com/2009/08/setting-a-lamp-test-environment-in-ubuntu-linux/
	In-text	(Garfield, 2007) or (Garfield, 2007, January 29)
		(Zaidi, 2009)
		(Jatin, 2009)

Podcast or video podcast (vodcast)	Reference list	Steinmetz, F. (Writer). (2009, October 2). Suicide notes, written by an alien mind [Audio podcast]. P. Rossi (Reader). In *Pseudopod: The sound of horror.* Retrieved from http://pseudopod.org/2009/10/02 /pseudopod-162-suicide-notes-written-by -an-alien-mind/
		▸ Or to avoid the long URL:
		Steinmetz, F. (Writer). (2009, October 2). Suicide notes, written by an alien mind [Audio podcast]. P. Rossi (Reader). In *Pseudopod: The sound of horror.* Retrieved from http://pseudopod.org/
		2057: Human civilization. (2006, December 27) [Video podcast]. Retrieved from http:// dsc.discovery.com/videos/2057-human -civilization.html
		▸ Or
		Kaku, M. (Host). (2006, December 27). 2057: Human civilization [Video podcast]. Retrieved from http://dsc.discovery.com /videos/2057-human-civilization.html
	In-text	(Steinmetz, 2009)
		("2057," 2006)
		▸ Or
		(Kaku, 2006)
Social networking site (Facebook, MySpace, Twitter)	Reference list	Simpson, M. [Maggie]. (n.d.) [Profile]. Retrieved from http://www.myspace.com/maggie simpson
		▸ When initials are not enough (in this case, let's pretend Marge happened to be listed as an author in the references also), add a first name in square brackets. In text, cite the full name.
		Obama, B. (2009, October 20). [Comment.] Retrieved from http://www.facebook.com /barackobama
		O'Neal, S. (2009, October 20, 1:22 p.m.). [Comment]. Retrieved from http://twitter .com/THE_REAL_SHAQ

	In-text	(Maggie Simpson, n.d.) (Obama, 2009) (O'Neal, 2009)

E-mail and text messages, instant messages (chat), and electronic mailing lists or discussion groups	Reference list	▸ Personal e-mails, text and other instant messages, and non-archived messages to mailing lists or discussion groups are not included in the reference list because they cannot be retrieved by third parties. You should include items that can be accessed through a URL. Quigley, M. (2009, September 30). National Council on Disability calls for health care reform for people with disabilities [Electronic mailing list message]. National Council on Disability News List (NCD-NEWS-L). Retrieved from http://listserv .access.gpo.gov/ ▸ If the name of the group or list is not evident from the URL, you must include it in the reference.
	In-text	(Quigley, 2009) ▸ Because personal e-mails and instant messages are not included in the reference list, they should be fully described in the text. (E. Leis, e-mail message to author, 2007, May 3) (M. H. Lipson, instant message to J. S. Lipson, 2009, March 9) ▸ You may include the time of an electronic message if it is important or differentiates it from others. For example: (M. H. Lipson, instant message to J. S. Lipson, 2009, March 9, 11:23 a.m.)

APA does not permit very many abbreviations in its reference lists. When it does, it sometimes wants them capitalized and sometimes not. Who knows why?

APA: COMMON ABBREVIATIONS IN REFERENCE LISTS

chapter	chap.	part	Pt.
edition	ed.	revised edition	Rev. ed.
editor	Ed.	second edition	2nd ed.
no date	n.d.	supplement	Suppl.
number	No.	translated by	Trans.
page	p.	volume	Vol. (e.g., Vols. 2–5)
pages	pp.	volumes	vols. (e.g., 3 vols.)

6 AAA CITATIONS FOR ANTHROPOLOGY AND ETHNOGRAPHY

The American Anthropological Association (AAA) has designed its own citation style for the discipline. Within the text, citations use a standard author-date format, such as (Fogelson 2007) or (Comaroff and Comaroff 2008). That's the same as the familiar APA system (minus the comma). The difference comes at the end of the paper, in References Cited. Here, the anthropology system places the author's name on a separate line and lists all the publications below it, in a special indented form. (It's a hanging indent so the date of publication stands out.) For example:

Humphrey, Caroline
 2006 On Being Named and Not Named: Authority, Persons, and Their Names in Mongolia. *In* The Anthropology of Names and Naming. Gabriele vom Bruck, Barbara Bodenhorn, ed. Pp. 157–176. Cambridge: Cambridge University Press.
Sahlins, Marshall
 2000a Ethnographic Experience and Sentimental Pessimism: Why Culture Is Not a Disappearing Object. *In* Biographies of Scientific Objects. Lorraine Daston, ed. Pp. 158–293. Chicago: University of Chicago Press.
 2000b Waiting for Foucault. 3rd edition. Chicago: Prickly Paradigm Press.
 2004 Apologies to Thucydides: Understanding History as Culture and Vice Versa. Chicago: University of Chicago Press.

List the earliest works first. If an author has published more than one work in the same year, as Sahlins has for 2000, list them in alphabetical order and mark them "a," "b," and "c." If Sahlins has a coauthor, list that pairing on a separate line (as if they were a new author), below Sahlins as a single author.

Within the text, keep citations as simple as possible. That may be the author's name and the year of publication, such as (Silverstein 2008). If the sentence already includes the author's name, the citation can be even simpler:

Kelly (2011) offers a sophisticated argument on this point.

It is easy to include specific pages if you want to reference them. For example:

Kelly (2011:9–13) offers a sophisticated argument on this point.

You'll often want to include pages like this, and you'll need to when you quote an author.

The table below shows how to use AAA citations across a wide range of items. If you want more information, you can find it online at

- http://www.aaanet.org/publications/style_guide.pdf

You can also find examples of citations using AAA style in the association's official journal, *American Anthropologist*.

Although AAA citations are always made with author-date references (in parentheses), your text may also include some explanatory notes. These footnotes or endnotes can be used to discuss supplementary issues; they cannot be used for citations. If you need to cite something within the note itself, simply use author-date references in parentheses, as you would elsewhere.

INDEX OF AAA CITATIONS IN THIS CHAPTER

AAA: REFERENCES CITED AND IN-TEXT CITATIONS

Book, one author	References Cited	Silverman, Marilyn 2005 Ethnography and Development: The Work of Richard F. Salisbury. Montreal: McGill-Queen's. Boddy, Janice 2007 Civilizing Women: British Crusades in Colonial Sudan. Princeton: Princeton University Press. ▶ Book titles are not italicized. ▶ Do not include state abbreviations for reasonably well-known cities.
	In-text	(Silverman 2005) (Boddy 2007) or, for specific pages or chapters: (Boddy 2007:41) (Boddy 2007, ch. 4)
Books, several by same author	References Cited	Doniger, Wendy 2000 The Bedtrick: Tales of Sex and Masquerade. Chicago: University of Chicago Press. 2004 Bed as Autobiography: A Visual Exploration of John Ransom Phillips. Chicago: Clarissa. 2005 The Woman Who Pretended to Be Who She Was: Myths of Self-Imitation. New York: Oxford University Press. Doniger, Wendy, and Gregory Spinner 1998 Misconceptions: Female Imaginations and Male Fantasies in Parental Imprinting. Daedalus 127(1):97–130.

> Publications from the earliest year are listed first, whether they are books or articles. When the same author or coauthors have several publications in the same year, list them alphabetically (by the first significant word in the title). Label them as "a," "b," and "c."
> Coauthored books and articles follow a writer's single-author ones, in the alphabetical order of the second author's surname.
> Books and articles are listed under an author's name only if they all have exactly the same author (or authors). Thus, the publications listed under Doniger do not include others written jointly with Gregory Spinner.

	In-text	(Doniger 2000, 2004, 2005) (Doniger and Spinner 1998)

Book, multiple authors	References Cited	Weber, Gerhard W., and Fred L. Bookstein
		  2007 Virtual Anthropology: A Guide to a New Interdisciplinary Field. New York: Springer.
		Norberg-Hodge, Helena, Todd Merrifield, and Steven Gorelick
		  2002 Bringing the Food Economy Home: Local Alternatives to Global Agribusiness. London: Zed.
		▸ AAA says to include *all* authors' names.

	In-text	(Weber and Bookstein 2007) (Norberg-Hodge et al. 2002) ▸ Name up to two authors. For three or more, name only the first one and then use "et al."

Book, multiple editions	References Cited	Hockings, Paul, ed.
		  2004 Principles of Visual Anthropology. 3rd edition. Berlin: Mouton de Gruyter.
		Peacock, James L.
		  2001 The Anthropological Lens. Rev. edition. Cambridge: Cambridge University Press.
		▸ To differentiate the English and American university towns:

Cambridge: Cambridge University Press.
Cambridge, MA: Harvard University Press.

	In-text	(Hockings 2004) (Peacock 2001) ▶ To refer to a specific page for a quotation: (Peacock 2001:12)

Book, multiple editions, corporate author	References Cited	American Psychological Association
		  2010 Publication Manual of the American
		    Psychological Association. 6th edition.
		    Washington, DC: American Psychological
		    Association.

	In-text	(American Psychological Association [APA] 2010) ▶ Subsequent references are (APA 2010).

Book, anonymous or no author	References Cited	Anonymous
		  2003 Golden Verses of the Pythagoreans.
		    Whitefish, MT: Kessinger.

	In-text	(Anonymous 2003)

Book, edited	References Cited	Moore, Henrietta L., and Todd Sanders, eds.
		  2006 Anthropology in Theory: Issues
		    in Epistemology. Malden, MA: Blackwell.
		Vertovec, Steven, and Robin Cohen, eds.
		  2002 Conceiving Cosmopolitanism: Theory,
		    Context and Practice. Oxford: Oxford
		    University Press.

	In-text	(Moore and Sanders 2006) (Vertovec and Cohen 2002)

Book, online	References Cited	Klepinger, Linda L.
		  2006 Fundamentals of Forensic
		    Anthropology. Hoboken, NJ: John
		    Wiley & Sons. http://www.wiley
		    .com/WileyCDA/WileyTitle/product
		    Cd-0470007710,descCd-ebook
		    .html, accessed May 5, 2010.

	In-text	(Klepinger 2006)

Multivolume work	References Cited	Stocking, George W., Jr., ed.
		1983–96 History of Anthropology. 8 vols.
		Madison: University of Wisconsin Press.
		▸ AAA abbreviates inclusive years but not other types of number ranges.
	In-text	(Stocking 1983–96)

Single volume in a multivolume work	References Cited	Peregrine, Peter N., and Melvin Ember, eds.
		2001 Encyclopedia of Prehistory, vol. 6: North America. New York: Kluwer Academic/ Plenum Publishers.
		Stocking, George W., Jr.
		1991 History of Anthropology, vol. 7: Colonial Situations: Essays on the Contextualization of Ethnographic Knowledge. George W. Stocking Jr., ed. Madison: University of Wisconsin Press.
	In-text	(Peregrine and Ember 2001)
		(Stocking 1991)

Book in a series	References Cited	Whittaker, Andrea
		2004 Abortion, Sin and the State in Thailand. ASAA Women in Asia Series. New York: Routledge.
		Posey, Darrell A.
		2004 Indigenous Knowledge and Ethics: A Darrell Posey Reader. Kristina Plenderleith, ed. Studies in Environmental Anthropology, 10. New York: Routledge.
	In-text	(Whittaker 2004)
		(Posey 2004)

Reprint of earlier edition	References Cited	Boas, Franz
		2004[1932] Anthropology and Modern Life. New Brunswick, NJ: Transaction.
		▸ AAA doesn't put a space between the two dates.

	In-text	(Boas 2004) or for a specific page (Boas 2004:43) ▸ In-text citations use only the reprint date.

Translated
volume
	References
	Cited
		Foucault, Michel
		    1977 Discipline and Punish: The Birth of the
		        Prison. Alan Sheridan, trans. New York:
		        Pantheon.

	In-text	(Foucault 1977)

Chapter in
edited book
	References
	Cited
		Silverstein, Michael
		    2000 Whorfianism and the Linguistic
		        Imagination of Nationality. *In* Regimes
		        of Language: Ideologies, Polities, and
		        Identities. Paul V. Kroskrity, ed. Pp. 85–138.
		        Santa Fe, NM: School of American Research
		        Press.
		▸ Chapter titles are not placed in quotes or
		    italicized.
		Deming, Alison Hawthorne
		    2007 Where Time and Place Are Lost. *In*
		        Landscapes with Figures: The Nonfiction of
		        Place. Robert Root, ed. Pp. 34–41. Lincoln:
		        Bison Books, University of Nebraska.
		▸ Forewords, introductions, and afterwords
		    are treated the same way, with pagination
		    immediately before the place of publication.

	In-text	(Silverstein 2000) (Deming 2007)

Journal
article,
one
author
	References
	Cited
		Fischer, Michael M. J.
		    2007 Culture and Cultural Analysis
		        as Experimental Systems. Current
		        Anthropology 22:1–65.
		▸ Article titles are not placed in quotes; journal
		    titles are not italicized.
		▸ There's no need to name a specific issue if the
		    journal pages are numbered continuously
		    throughout the volume. However, if each issue
		    begins with page 1, then the issue's number
		    or month is necessary to find the article:
		    22(1):1–65.

Jordt, Ingrid
  2003 From Relations of Power to Relations
        of Authority: Epistemic Claims, Practices
        and Ideology in the Production of Burma's
        Political Order. Theme issue, "Knowledge
        and Verification," Social Analysis
        47(1):65–76.
Robinson, Kathryn
  2006 Islamic Influences on Indonesian
        Feminism. Social Analysis 50(1):171–177.

In-text (Fischer 2007)
         (Jordt 2003)
         (Robinson 2006)

| Journal article, multiple authors | References Cited | Beck, Robin A., Jr., David G. Moore, and Christopher B. Rodning
  2006 Identifying Fort San Juan: A Sixteenth-Century Spanish Occupation at the Berry Site, North Carolina. Southeastern Archaeology 25:65–77.
▸ Name all authors in the References Cited. |
| | In-text | (Beck et al. 2006) for more than two authors |

Journal article, online

References Cited

Smith, Alexia, and Natalie D. Munro
  2009 A Holistic Approach to Examining
        Ancient Agriculture: A Case Study from the
        Bronze and Iron Age Near East. Current
        Anthropology 50(6):925–936. doi:10.1086
        /648316, accessed May 5, 2010.
Mitchell, Timothy
  2002 McJihad: Islam in the U.S. Global
        Order. Social Text 20(4):1–18. doi:10.1215
        /01642472-20-4_73-1, accessed May 5, 2010.
▸ Many journal articles assign a Digital Object
  Identifier (DOI). A DOI—a permanent ID—is
  preferable to a URL. (Pasting the DOI into a
  DOI resolver, available from CrossRef.org, will
  direct you to the article—wherever it is posted.)
  If you don't see a DOI, list the URL (the address
  in your browser's location bar). For overly long
  URLs, list the home page of the journal, journal
  issue, or database.

Appelbaum, Richard P.
   1979 Born-Again Functionalism? A
   Reconsideration of Althusser's
   Structuralism. Critical Sociology 9(1):18–33.
   http://crs.sagepub.com/content/vol9
   /issue1/, accessed May 5, 2010.

	In-text	(Smith and Munro 2009) (Mitchell 2002) (Appelbaum 1979)

Newspaper
or magazine
article, no
author
	References
	Cited
		Economist
		  2007 Haiti: Building a Reluctant Nation.
		     Economist, February 10: 35.
		New York Times
		  2003 Strong Aftershocks Continue in
		     California. New York Times, December 26:
		     A23, national edition.

	In-text	(*Economist* 2007) ▸ Titles used in place of authors are italicized in the text but not in the References Cited. ▸ For multiple citations to 2007: (*Economist* 2007a) (*New York Times* 2003) or if necessary: (*New York Times* 2003a)

Newspaper
or magazine
article, with
author
	References
	Cited
		Vogel, Carol
		  2009 Prices Far Surpass Estimates at
		     Sotheby's Auction. New York Times,
		     November 5: A31, New York edition.

	In-text	(Vogel 2009) ▸ For multiple citations to author in 2009: (Vogel 2009a)

Newspaper
or magazine
article, online
	References
	Cited
		Copans, Laurie
		  2007 Clashes by Jerusalem Holy Site
		     Continue. Washington Post, February 10.
		     http://www.washingtonpost.com
		     /wp-dyn/content/article/2007/02/10
		     /AR2007021000544.html, accessed May 5,
		     2010.

Demetriou, Danielle

2007 Inca Link Is a Bridge Too Far, Say Critics. Daily Telegraph (London), February 10. http://www.telegraph.co.uk/travel /740155/Inca-link-is-a-bridge-too-far -say-critics.html, accessed May 5, 2010.

▸ If you're citing a commercial database, you can include an accession number after the URL for the home page. For example:

Cohn, Jonathan

2009 Party Is Such Sweet Sorrow. New Republic, September 23: 12. http:// www.proquest.com/ (Document ID: 1867667291), accessed May 5, 2010.

In-text	(Copans 2007) or (Copans 2007a) (Copans 2007b) (Demetriou 2007) or (Demetriou 2007a) (Cohn 2009) or (Cohn 2009a)

Review	References Cited	Banville, John 2007 *Review of* House of Meetings. New York Review of Books 54 (March 1): 38–40. http:// www.nybooks.com/, accessed May 5, 2010. Heffernan, Virginia 2007 The Gangs of Los Angeles: Roots, Branches and Bloods. *Review of* Bastards of the Party. Cle Sloan, dir. *In* New York Times. http://movies.nytimes.com/2007/02/06 /arts/television/06heff.html, accessed May 5, 2010. Blackburn, Simon 2007 *Review of* Descartes: The Life and Times of a Genius. *In* New York Times Book Review, February 4.
	In-text	(Banville 2007) (Heffernan 2007) (Blackburn 2007)

Exhibition catalog	References Cited	Smith, Joel 2006 Saul Steinberg: Illuminations. Exhibition catalog. New Haven, CT: Yale University Press.

	In-text	(Smith 2006)

| Unpublished paper, thesis, or dissertation | References Cited | Neill, Dawn
  2007 Land Insecurity, Urbanization, and Educational Investment among Indo-Fijians. Paper presented at the Annual Meeting of the Society for Applied Anthropology, Tampa Bay, FL, March 28.
Prough, Jennifer
  2006 Reading Culture, Engendering Girls: Politics of the Everyday in the Production of Girls' Manga. Ph.D. dissertation, Department of Cultural Anthropology, Duke University.
Brenneis, Donald
  N.d. Reforming Promise. Unpublished MS, Department of Anthropology, University of California, Santa Cruz.
  ▶ "MS" is in caps without a period.
Marlowe, Frank W.
  In press Mate Preferences among Hadza Hunter-Gatherers. Human Nature.
  ▶ This refers to a work accepted for publication. |
| | In-text | (Neill 2007)
(Prough 2006)
(Brenneis n.d.)
(Marlowe in press) |

| Microfilm, microfiche | References Cited | U.S. House of Representatives
  1871 First Report. Southern Claims Commission. Records (1871–1880). Microfilm Publication P2257, Frames 0145–0165. Washington, DC: National Archives.
Conservative Party (UK) Archive
  1919 Annual Report of the Executive Committee to Central Council. March 11–November 18. Microfiche card 143. Woodbridge, CT: Gale/Primary Source Microfilm, 1998. (Original material located in Conservative Party Archive, Bodleian Library, Oxford, UK.) |

▸ You do not need to include the location of the original material, but you are welcome to.

In-text	(U.S. House 1871) (Conservative Party 1919)

Archival
materials and
manuscript
collections,
hard copies
and online
	References
	Cited
		Rice Ballard Papers
		 N.d. Southern Historical Collection. Wilson
		  Library, University of North Carolina, Chapel
		  Hill.

▸ Or

Franklin, Isaac
  1831 Letter to R. C. Ballard, February 28. *In*
    Rice Ballard Papers, Southern Historical
    Collection. Wilson Library, University of
    North Carolina, Chapel Hill.

▸ In the text or explanatory notes, you may cite directly to Isaac Franklin's letter to R. C. Ballard and include it in your References Cited. Or you may refer to the letter in the text and cite to the collection (Rice Ballard Papers).

Boston YWCA Papers
  N.d. Schlesinger Library, Radcliffe Institute
    for Advanced Study, Harvard University.

▸ Or

Lamson, Mary Swift
  1891 An Account of the Beginning of the
    B.Y.W.C.A. MS [n.d.] and accompanying
    letter. Boston YWCA Papers. Schlesinger
    Library, Radcliffe Institute for Advanced
    Study, Harvard University.

▸ If Lamson's account is the only item cited from these papers, then it would be listed in the References Cited.

Taft, Horatio Nelson
  1861–62 Diary. Vol. 1, January 1, 1861–April 11,
    1862. Manuscript Division, Library of
    Congress. http://memory.loc.gov/ammem
    /tafthtml/tafthome.html, accessed
    May 5, 2010.

In-text:	(Rice Ballard Papers n.d.) (Boston YWCA Papers n.d.)

(Lamson 1891)
(Taft 1861–62)

Encyclopedia, hard copy and online	References Cited	Encyclopaedia Britannica 1987 Balkans: History. 15th edition. Vol. 14. Pp. 570–588. Chicago: Encyclopaedia Britannica. 2007 Balkans. http://www.britannica.com/EBchecked/topic/50325/Balkans, accessed May 5, 2010. Brumfiel, Elizabeth M. 2001 States and Civilizations, Archaeology of. *In* International Encyclopedia of Social and Behavioral Sciences. N. J. Smelser and P. B. Baltes, eds. Pp. 14983–14988. Oxford: Elsevier Science. Graham, George 2007 Behaviorism. *In* Stanford Encyclopedia of Philosophy. http://plato.stanford.edu/entries/behaviorism/, accessed May 5, 2010. Haas, Jonathan 2001 Kayenta Anasazi. *In* Encyclopedia of Prehistory: North America, vol. 6. Peter N. Peregrine and Melvin Ember, eds. Pp. 40–42. New York: Kluwer Academic/Plenum Publishers.
	In-text	(Encyclopaedia Britannica 1987) (Encyclopaedia Britannica 2007) (Brumfiel 2001) (Graham 2007) (Haas 2001)
Reference book, hard copy and online	References Cited	Pendergast, Sara, and Tom Pendergast, eds. 2003 Reference Guide to World Literature. 3rd edition. 2 vols. Detroit: St. James Press. Pendergast, Sara, and Tom Pendergast, eds. 2003 Reference Guide to World Literature. 3rd edition. Gale Virtual Reference Library. Detroit: Thomson/Gale. E-book.

Colman, Andrew M.

2001 A Dictionary of Psychology. Oxford: Oxford University Press. http://www .oxfordreference.com/, accessed May 5, 2010.

Obama Marks Holocaust in Germany, D-Day in France

2009 Facts On File World News Digest database. June 11. Accession no. 2009492010.

In-text	(Pendergast and Pendergast 2003)

► For a specific page in a specific volume:

(Pendergast and Pendergast 2003, vol. 2:619)

(Colman 2001)

("Obama Marks Holocaust" 2009)

Dictionary, hard copy, online, and CD-ROM	References Cited	Merriam-Webster's Collegiate Dictionary

2003 Caste. 11th edition. Springfield, MA: Merriam-Webster.

Compact Edition of the Oxford English Dictionary

1971 Protest, v. Oxford: Oxford University Press. Vol. 2:2335.

► The word "protest" is both a noun and a verb. Here, I am citing the verb.

Dictionary.com Unabridged

n.d. Class, n. http://dictionary.reference .com/browse/class, accessed May 5, 2010.

American Heritage Dictionary of the English Language

2000 Folklore. 4th edition. Boston: Houghton Mifflin. CD-ROM.

Speake, Jennifer, ed.

2003 "Where MacGregor sits is the head of the table." *In* Oxford Dictionary of Proverbs. 4th edition. P. 161. Oxford: Oxford University Press.

Winthrop, Robert H.

1991 Caste. *In* Dictionary of Concepts in Cultural Anthropology. Pp. 27–30. New York: Greenwood.

	In-text	(*Merriam-Webster's Collegiate Dictionary* 2003)
		(*Compact Edition of the Oxford English Dictionary* 1971)
		(*Dictionary.com Unabridged* n.d.)
		(*American Heritage Dictionary* 2000)
		▸ Titles used in place of authors are italicized in the text but not in the References Cited.
		(Speake 2003)
		(Winthrop 1991)
Speech, academic talk, or course lecture	References Cited	Bilsborough, Alan
		2006 Species, Pattern and Adaptation in Human Evolution. Presidential address, Royal Anthropological Institute, Canterbury, Eng., November 3.
		Comaroff, John L.
		2007 Course lecture. University of Chicago, Chicago, April 12.
	In-text	(Bilsborough 2006)
		(Comaroff 2007)
Interview	References Cited	Wilson, E. O.
		2007 Personal interview regarding evolution. Cambridge, MA, February 1.
		Douglas, Mary
		2003 Interview with John Clay. http://www .bhag.net/int/intdougm/intdougm_inte .html, accessed May 5, 2010.
		▸ Unpublished personal communications are often identified parenthetically in the text, such as (John Doe, interview with author, May 1, 2008). Some authors include communications like this in References Cited; some don't. AAA seems to be of two minds. Their online style guide says to omit them, but articles in their official journals frequently include them. My suggestion: it's your choice, but be consistent and definitely include communications that can be accessed by your readers, such as items posted online.

	In-text	(Wilson 2007) (Douglas 2003)
Television program	References Cited	Moore, Steven Dean, dir. 2002 Bart vs. Lisa vs. 3rd Grade. The Simpsons. Fox, November 17. ▸ To emphasize the title, a writer, or a particular actor, put that name on the top line (and include the director in the line below): Long, Tim, writer 2002 Bart vs. Lisa vs. 3rd Grade. Steven Dean Moore, dir. The Simpsons. Fox, November 17.
	In-text	(Moore 2002) (Long 2002)
Film	References Cited	Apted, Michael, dir. 2006 Amazing Grace. 111 min. Samuel Goldwyn Films. Hollywood. Asch, Timothy, and Napoleon Chagnon, creators 1975 The Ax Fight. 30 min. Black-and-white. National Anthropological Archives and Human Studies Film Archives, SA-81.5.1. ▸ Or to emphasize the title rather than the creators: Ax Fight, The 1975 Timothy Asch and Napoleon Chagnon, creators. 30 min. Black-and-white. National Anthropological Archives and Human Studies Film Archives, SA-81.5.1. ▸ Films may be included in the References Cited or may be listed separately in a section entitled "Filmography References" or "Films Cited."
	In-text	(Apted 2006) (Asch and Chagnon 1975) or (*Ax Fight* 1975)
Photograph	References Cited	Adams, Ansel 1927 Monolith, the Face of Half Dome, Yosemite National Park. Photograph. Chicago: Art Institute.

▸ Or if you used a photograph online:

Adams, Ansel

  1927 Monolith, the Face of Half Dome,
    Yosemite National Park. Photograph.
    Chicago: Art Institute. http://www.hctc
    .commnet.edu/artmuseum/anseladams
    /details/pdf/monlith.pdf, accessed
    May 5, 2010.

▸ Photographs are seldom included in reference
lists. They are usually identified in the article
itself, immediately beneath the photo. For
example, a photo of rural houses might include
this explanation: Typical sharecropper homes,
Quitman County, Mississippi (January 2008)
(Photo by Maude Schuyler Clay)

In-text	(Adams 1927)

Figures: map, chart, graph, or table	Credit or explanation for figure or table	▸ Give a descriptive title to your maps, charts, photos, graphs, and tables. Place an identifying credit or clarifying information below the item, such as:

Dancing at Carnival, Rio de Janeiro (2008)
(Photo by Eric Cartman)

President James Knox Polk, three-quarter-length
portrait (1849) (Daguerreotype by Mathew
Brady) (Collection of the Library of Congress)

Ceremonial grave markers (Mohawk)
(Collection of Art Institute of Chicago)

All figures in this table are rounded to nearest
percentile.

Two-tailed significance tests: $*p < .05$ $**p < .01$

▸ You may also need to list sources for a figure,
map, chart, graph, or table. Here, for example,
is a title for a table, with an asterisk after the
title to identify the sources of information
on which it is based. These sources (Jones
and Smith) are identified by in-text citations
on a line below the table. Full information
about them appears in the References Cited.

Table 4: Fertility rates of Bedouins in Israel*
*Sources: Jones (2007), Smith (2008)

Musical recording	References Cited	Johnson, Robert 1961 Cross Road Blues. *From* Robert Johnson: King of the Delta Blues Singers. New York: Columbia Records.
	In-text	(Johnson 1961)
Sound recording	References Cited	Doniger, Wendy 2003 The Essential Kamasutra. 5-CD set. Boulder, CO: Sounds True.
	In-text	(Doniger 2003)

Government document, hard copy and online	References Cited	U.S. Senate, Committee on Armed Services
		    1947 Hearings on S. 758: A bill to promote the national security by providing for a national defense establishment. 80th Cong., 1st sess.
		U.S. Bureau of the Census
		    2007 Statistical Abstracts of the U.S. Washington, DC: U.S. Bureau of the Census.
		Federal Trade Commission
		    2006 How to Buy Genuine American Indian Arts and Crafts. http://www.doi.gov/iacb /brochures/indianartftc.pdf, accessed May 5, 2010.
		UN Development Programme
		    2009 Human Development Report 2009: Overcoming Barriers: Human Mobility and Development. http://hdr.undp.org/en /reports/global/hdr2009/, accessed May 5, 2010.

	In-text	(U.S. Senate, Committee on Armed Services 1947) (U.S. Bureau of the Census 2007) (Federal Trade Commission 2006) (UN Development Programme 2009)
Database	References Cited	ARD: The Anthropology Review Database N.d. Hugh Jarvis, ed. http://wings.buffalo.edu /anthropology/ARD/, accessed May 5, 2010.

National Archeological Database
2008 NADB Reports. http://www.cast
.uark.edu/other/nps/nadb/nadb.mul
.html, accessed May 5, 2010.

	In-text	(ARD n.d.)
		(National Archeological Database 2008)

Website or web page	References Cited	Digital History

N.d. Sidney Mintz, ed. http://www
.digitalhistory.uh.edu/, accessed May 5,
2010.
Internet Public Library (IPL)
2009 University of Michigan/Drexel
University. http://www.ipl.org/, accessed
May 5, 2010.
Harvard University, Department of
Anthropology
2009 Home page. http://www.fas.harvard
.edu/~anthro/, accessed May 5, 2010.
▶ If a website or web page does not show a date
when it was copyrighted or updated, then list
"N.d." where the year normally appears.

	In-text	(Digital History n.d.)
		(Internet Public Library 2007) or (IPL 2007)
		(Harvard University, Dept. of Anthropology 2007)

Blog, entry or comment	References Cited	Drezner, Daniel W.

2009 Drezner, Daniel W. A Dangerous
Moment of Foreign Policy Fatigue. Blog
post, October 29. http://drezner
.foreignpolicy.com/posts/2009/10/29
/a_dangerous_moment_of_foreign_policy
_fatigue, accessed May 5, 2010.
"Rex" (Alex Golub)
2009 Additional Coverage of Lévi-Strauss.
Blog post, November 5. Savage Minds:
Notes and Queries in Anthropology.
http://savageminds.org/2009/11/05
/additional-coverage-of-levi-strauss/,
accessed May 5, 2010.

lurking

> 2009　Response to "Rex," Additional
> Coverage of Lévi-Strauss. Savage Minds:
> Notes and Queries in Anthropology.
> http://savageminds.org/2009/11/05
> /additional-coverage-of-levi-strauss
> /#comment-622734, accessed May 5, 2010.

In-text

(Drezner 2009)

("Rex" 2009)

(lurking 2009)

7 CSE CITATIONS FOR THE BIOLOGICAL SCIENCES

CSE citations, devised by the Council of Science Editors, are widely used for scientific papers, journals, and books in the life sciences. The citations are based on international principles adopted by the National Library of Medicine.

Actually, the CSE system lets you choose among three ways of citing documents:

- *Citation-sequence:* Citations are numbered (1), (2), (3), in the order they appear in the text. Full references appear at the end of the paper—in the same order. They are *not* alphabetized.
- *Citation-name:* Citations are numbered, with full references at the end of the paper—in alphabetical order. The first item cited in the text might be number 8 on the alphabetical list. It would be cited as (8), even though it appeared first—and (8) if it appears again.
- *Name-year:* Citations in the text are given as name and year, such as (McClintock 2006). Full references appear at the end of the paper in alphabetical order, just as they do in APA citations.

Whichever format you choose, use it consistently throughout the paper. Ask your instructor which one she prefers.

Citation-sequence: Cite the first reference in the text as number 1, the second as number 2, and so on. You can use brackets [1], superscripts[1], or parentheses (1). At the end of the paper, list all the items, beginning with the first one cited. The list is *not* alphabetical. If the first item you cite is by Professor Zangwill, then that's the first item in the reference list. If you cite Zangwill's paper again, it's still [1], even if it's the last citation in your paper. If you want to cite several items at once, simply include the number for each one, separated by commas, such as [1,3,9] or [1,3,9] or (1,3,9). If items have successive numbers, use hyphens: 4–6,12–18.

Citation-name: Begin by assembling an alphabetical list of references at the end of the text and numbering them. Each item in the list will have a number, which is used whenever that book or article is cited in the text. If the Zangwill article is thirty-sixth in the alphabetical list, then it is always cited with that number, even if it's the first item you cite in the paper. The next reference in the text might be [23], the one after that might be [12]. Citations can be set as superscripts, in brackets, or in parentheses. If you want to cite several items at once, include a number for each one, such as [4,15,22] or [4,15,22] or (4,15,22). Use hyphens for continuous numbers (1–3). So a citation could be (4,16–18,22).

Name-year: For in-text citations, use the (name-year) format without commas, such as (Cronin and Siegler 2007) and (Siegler et al. 2008). The reference list is alphabetical by author and includes all cited articles. If an author has several articles, list the earliest ones first. Follow the same method if an author has published several articles in the same year. List the first one as 2008a, the second as 2008b, and so on by the month of publication. To cite several articles by Susan Lindquist, then, the notation might be (Lindquist 2007d, 2008a, 2008h), referring to those three articles in the reference list.

In the same way, you can also cite articles by different authors within the same reference. Separate them by semicolons, such as (Liebman 2007; Ma and Lindquist 2008; Outeiro and Lindquist 2008).

If the author's name appears in the sentence, you do not need to repeat it in the citation. For example, "According to LaBarbera (2010), this experiment . . ."

What if LaBarbera had ten or fifteen coauthors? That's certainly possible in the sciences. Articles sometimes have dozens of authors because they include everyone involved in the experiments leading to publication. My colleague Henry Frisch, a high-energy physicist, told me that one of his articles has nearly eight hundred coauthors![1] I grew up in a town with a smaller phone book. Really.

How many of these authors should you include when you use name-year citations in the text? Don't go overboard. Just list the first seven hundred. If you do that in the first sentence, you'll reach the paper's word limit before you even have to write a second sentence. That's one easy science paper.

---

1. Professor Frisch's own practice is to list himself as author only if he actually helped write the paper. His practice is unusual, but a number of scientists think he's right and that current practices are unclear and often lax. To correct the problem, some scientists are circulating proposals that would require coauthors to specify how they contributed to joint papers. For Frisch's comments on the metastasizing growth of coauthors, see his web page, http://hep.uchicago.edu/~frisch.

Actually, CSE offers clear recommendations, stopping a bit short of seven hundred authors. If there are only two authors, list them both, separated by "and." If there are three or more authors, list only the first one, followed by "et al." For example: (LaBarbera et al. 2010). Later, I'll show you how to handle coauthors in the reference list at the end of the paper.

QUICK COMPARISON OF CSE STYLES

Style	In-text citations	Reference list at end of paper
Citation-sequence	(1), (2), (3), (4)	Items listed in order of their text appearance
Citation-name	(31), (2), (13), (7)	Items listed alphabetically, by author surname
Name-year	(Shapiro 2008)	Items listed alphabetically, by author surname

STYLES OF REFERENCE LISTS

All three styles require reference lists following the text. CSE emphasizes brevity and simplicity for these lists. Instead of using the authors' first names, use only their initials. Omit periods after the initials and don't put spaces between them: Stern HK.

Shorten journal names with standard abbreviations, such as those listed in the PubMed journals database available at http://www.ncbi.nlm .nih.gov/journals. CSE doesn't use periods in shortening journal titles. So, J Biosci Bioeng (without periods) is the abbreviation for the *Journal of Bioscience and Bioengineering*.

CSE uses sentence-style capitalization for titles. Capitalize only the first word, proper nouns, and the first word after a colon. Format the titles in normal type rather than italics.

If you cite something you've read online rather than in print, cite the electronic version. After all, the two versions may differ. To do that, CSE style requires you to add a couple of items to the citation: (1) the date you accessed the document and (2) the fact that it was an Internet document. In the citation, you should insert [Internet] in square brackets, immediately after the journal title, and the date you accessed it; then, after the article's pagination, insert the URL.

Print citation   Csaba G, Pállinger É. 2009. Effect of stress and stress hormones on the hormone (insulin) binding of Tetrahymena. Cell Biochem Funct. 27:448–451.

Internet citation	Csaba G, Pállinger É. 2009. Effect of stress and stress hormones on the hormone (insulin) binding of Tetrahymena. Cell Biochem Funct [Internet]. [cited 2009 May 5]; 27:448–451. Available from: http://www3.interscience.wiley.com/journal/122591096/abstract

If you wish to include a Digital Object Identifier (DOI) or a database accession number, put it last. There is no period after the DOI or accession number.

Internet citation with URL and DOI	Csaba G, Pállinger É. 2009. Effect of stress and stress hormones on the hormone (insulin) binding of Tetrahymena. Cell Biochem Funct [Internet]. [cited 2009 May 5]; 27:448–451. Available from: http://www3.interscience.wiley.com/journal/122591096/abstract. doi:10.1002/cbf.1592

This article, like nearly all printed articles, was not modified after it was published. But preprints are often modified and so are articles in electronic journals. You need to include that information in the citation so your readers will know which version you are citing. That information appears in the square brackets, immediately before the date you accessed the item.

Modified paper	Csaba G, Pállinger É. 2009. Effect of stress and stress hormones on the hormone (insulin) binding of Tetrahymena. Cell Biochem Funct [Internet]. [modified 2009 Sept 8; cited 2009 Sept 10]; 27:448–451. Available from: http://www3.interscience.wiley.com/journal/122591096/abstract. doi:10.1002/cbf.1592

Don't worry about remembering all these details. There are too many of them. I'll explain them in the tables that follow and include plenty of examples. If you use this style often, you'll gradually grow familiar with the fine points.

These tables show CSE recommendations for in-text citations and reference lists, using all three formats. Not every journal follows them exactly, so you'll see some variation as you read scientific publications. Journals differ, for example, in how many coauthors they include in the reference list. Some list only the first three authors before adding "et al." One lists the first twenty-six. (Imagine being poor coauthor number 27.) The CSE says to name up to ten and then add "et al."

These tables are based on Council of Science Editors, *Scientific Style and Format: The CSE Manual for Authors, Editors, and Publishers,* 7th ed. (Reston, VA: Council of Science Editors, 2006).

CSE: NAME-YEAR SYSTEM

Journal article	Reference list	Zheng M, McPeek MS. 2007. Multipoint linkage-disequilibrium mapping with haplotype-block structure. Am J Hum Genet. 80(1):112–125.

▸ CSE does not require the issue number for consecutively paginated journal volumes like this one, but it's always okay to include it.

Wong KK et al. 2007. A comprehensive analysis of common copy-number variations in the human genome. Am J Hum Genet. 80(1):91–104.

▸ The Wong article has eleven authors. CSE says to list the first ten, followed by "et al." But individual journals vary in their practice. Some would include all of them in the reference list. Most would include only the first two.

	In-text	(Zheng and McPeek 2007) (Wong et al. 2007)

▸ If your list includes several publications by Wong and other authors in 2007, your in-text reference should include coauthors to clarify exactly which article you are citing. For example: (Wong, deLeeuw et al. 2007).

Journal article, online	Reference list	Alvarez-Dolado M. 2007. Cell fusion: Biological perspectives and potential for regenerative medicine. Front Biosci [Internet]. [cited 2010 May 5]; 12:1–2. Available from: http://www .bioscience.org/

▸ This journal article is online only. Do *not* add a period at the end of the URL.

▸ Note the unusual way that dates are written in this CSE style: 2010 May 5.

	In-text	(Alvarez-Dolado 2007)

Abstract of article	Reference list	Erkut S, Uckan S. 2006. Alveolar distraction osteogenesis and implant placement in a severely resorbed maxilla: A clinical report [Abstract]. J Prosthet Dent. 95(5):340–343.

▶ CSE's 7th edition of *Style and Format* does not specify a style for citing abstracts. The format shown here is consistent, however, with other citation rules in that edition.

Erkut S, Uckan S. 2006. Alveolar distraction osteogenesis and implant placement in a severely resorbed maxilla: A clinical report. J Prosthet Dent. 95(5):340–343. In: Dent Abstr. 2007;52(1):17–19.

▶ The upper reference is to the abstract, as published in the article itself. The lower reference is to the abstract, published in a different journal.

In-text	(Erkut and Uckan 2006) (Erkut and Uckan 2006)

Book, one author	Reference list	Brereton RG. 2007. Applied chemometrics for scientists. Hoboken (NJ): John Wiley & Sons.
		Wiggins CE. 2007. A concise guide to orthopaedic and musculoskeletal impairment ratings. Philadelphia: Lippincott Williams & Wilkins. ▶ If the publisher's city is well known, you may omit the state.
	In-text	(Brereton 2007) (Wiggins 2007) ▶ To cite the same author for works written in several years: (Wiggins 2006, 2007a, 2007b, 2008) ▶ To cite works by authors with the same surname published in the same year, include the authors' initials: (Wiggins CE 2008; Wiggins LJ 2008)

Book, multiple authors	Reference list	Villas-Boas SG, Nielsen J, Smedsgaard J, Hansen MAE, Roessner-Tunali U. 2007. Metabolome analysis: An introduction. Hoboken (NJ): John Wiley & Sons. ▶ In the reference list, name up to ten authors, then add "et al."

	In-text	(Villas-Boas et al. 2007) ▸ If there are just two authors, name them both: (Villas-Boas and Nielsen 2008)
Book, multiple editions	Reference list	Tropp BE. 2007. Molecular biology: Genes to proteins. 3rd ed. Sudbury (MA): Jones and Bartlett.
		Snell RS. 2007. Clinical anatomy by regions. 8th ed. Philadelphia: Lippincott Williams & Wilkins. ▸ For a revised edition, the phrase "Rev. ed." appears where "8th ed." currently does.
	In-text	(Tropp 2007) (Snell 2007)
Book, multiple editions, no author	Reference list	Publication manual of the American Psychological Association. 2010. 6th ed. Washington (DC): American Psychological Association.
	In-text	(Publication manual . . . 2010) ▸ Do not use "Anonymous" in place of the author name. Instead, use the first word or first few words of the title and an ellipsis, followed by the date.
Book, edited	Reference list	Baluka F, Mancuso S, Volkmann D, editors. 2006. Communication in plants: Neuronal aspects of plant life. Berlin: Springer-Verlag.
	In-text	(Baluka et al. 2006)
Chapter in edited book	Reference list	Kelley SO. 2007. Nanowires for biomolecular sensing. In: Vo-Dinh T, editor. Nanotechnology in biology and medicine: Methods, devices, and applications. Boca Raton (FL): CRC Press/Taylor & Francis. p. 95–101.
	In-text	(Kelley 2007)

Preprint	Reference list	Prgomet M, Georgiou A, Westbrook J. 2009. The impact of mobile handheld technology on hospital physicians' work practices and patient care: A systematic review. Preprint. J Am Med Inform Assoc [Internet]. [cited 2009 Oct 8]. Available from: http://www.jamia.org/cgi /reprint/M3215v1. doi:10.1197/jamia.M3215
		▸ CSE's 7th edition of *Style and Format* does not specify a style for citing preprints. The format shown here is consistent, however, with other citations rules in that edition.
	In-text	(Prgomet et al. 2009)
Government document, hard copy or online	Reference list	Marinopoulos SS, Dorman T, Ratanawongsa N, Wilson LM, Ashar BH, Magaziner JL, Miller RG, Thomas PA, Prokopowicz GP, Qayyum R, et al. 2007. Effectiveness of continuing medical education. Rockville (MD): Agency for Healthcare Research and Quality. AHRQ Pub. No. 07-E006.
		[AHRQ] Agency for Healthcare Research and Quality. 2007. Testing for cytochrome P450 polymorphisms in adults with non-psychotic depression treated with selective serotonin reuptake inhibitors (SSRIs) [Structured Abstract]. Rockville (MD): AHRQ; [cited 2010 May 5]. AHRQ Pub. No. 07-E002. Available from: http://www.ahrq.gov/clinic/tp/cyp450tp.htm
		▸ If an organization is both author and publisher, the name may be abbreviated as publisher.
	In-text	(Marinopoulos et al. 2007) (AHRQ 2007)
CD-ROM or DVD	Reference list	3D human anatomy: Regional edition [DVD-ROM]. 2009. London (England): Primal Pictures.
	In-text	(3D human anatomy 2009)
Database	Reference list	RCSB Protein Data Bank [Internet]. 2010 [cited 2010 May 5]. Available from: http://www.rcsb .org/pdb/home/home.do

		[NIH] National Institutes of Health, Office of Dietary Supplements. 2010. International Bibliographic Information on Dietary Supplements (IBIDS) Database [Internet]. [cited 2010 May 5]. Available from: http://ods.od.nih.gov/Health_Information/IBIDS.aspx ▸ Both databases are continually updated. Rather than listing "[date unknown]," you can list the year from the "cited" date.
	In-text	(RCSB Protein Data Bank 2010) (NIH 2010) or (NIH IBIDS Database 2010)
Website or web page	Reference list	[CSE] Council of Science Editors. [date unknown]. Citing the Internet: Formats for bibliographic citation [Internet]. Reston (VA): Council of Science Editors; [cited 2010 May 5]. Available from: http://www.councilscienceeditors.org/publications/citing_internet.cfm ▸ Where this citation says only [Internet], yours might say [monograph on Internet] or [database on Internet]. [USDA] US Department of Agriculture, Agricultural Research Service. 2009. Home page [Internet]. Washington (DC): USDA; [cited 2009 Nov 8]. Available from: http://www.ars.usda.gov/main/main.htm [NLM] National Library of Medicine. [date unknown]. Bookshelf [Internet]. [cited 2010 May 5]. Available from: http://www.ncbi.nlm.nih.gov/sites/entrez?db=Books
	In-text	(CSE date unknown) (USDA 2009) (NLM date unknown)

The next table shows CSE references using citation-sequence and citation-name formats. The main difference from the previous table is that the date appears later in the reference. I have used the same examples, in case you want to compare formats.

CSE: CITATION-SEQUENCE AND CITATION-NAME SYSTEMS

Journal article	Reference list	Zheng M, McPeek MS. Multipoint linkage-disequilibrium mapping with haplotype-block structure. Am J Hum Genet. 2007;80(1):112–125.
		Wong KK, deLeeuw RJ, et al. A comprehensive analysis of common copy-number variations in the human genome. Am J Hum Genet. 2007;80(1):91–104.
Journal article, online	Reference list	Alvarez-Dolado M. Cell fusion: Biological perspectives and potential for regenerative medicine. Front Biosci [Internet]. 2007 [cited 2010 May 5]; 12:1–2. Available from: http://www.bioscience.org/ ▶ This journal article is online only.
Abstract	Reference list	▶ How you list an abstract depends on whether you are referring to: • An abstract included in the article itself • An abstract that appears in a different journal and that you are citing *without* reading the original article ▶ Abstract only, within the article itself: Erkut S, Uckan S. Alveolar distraction osteogenesis and implant placement in a severely resorbed maxilla: A clinical report [Abstract]. J Prosthet Dent. 2006;95(5):340–343. ▶ Abstract only, in a different journal from the article: Erkut S, Uckan S. Alveolar distraction osteogenesis and implant placement in a severely resorbed maxilla: A clinical report. J Prosthet Dent. 2006;95(5):340–343. In: Dent Abstr. 2007;52(1):17–19.
Book, one author	Reference list	Brereton RG. Applied chemometrics for scientists. Hoboken (NJ): John Wiley & Sons; 2007.
		Wiggins CE. A concise guide to orthopaedic and musculoskeletal impairment ratings. Philadelphia: Lippincott Williams & Wilkins; 2007.

> ► If the publisher's city is well known, you may omit the state abbreviation, if you wish.

Book, multiple authors	Reference list	Villas-Boas SG, Nielsen J, Smedsgaard J, Hansen MAE, Roessner-Tunali U. Metabolome analysis: An introduction. Hoboken (NJ): John Wiley & Sons; 2007. ► In the reference list, name up to ten authors, then add "et al."
Book, multiple editions	Reference list	Tropp BE. Molecular biology: Genes to proteins. 3rd ed. Sudbury (MA): Jones and Bartlett; 2007. Snell RS. Clinical anatomy by regions. 8th ed. Philadelphia: Lippincott Williams & Wilkins; 2007. ► For a revised edition, use "Rev. ed." in place of "8th ed."
Book, multiple editions, no author	Reference list	Publication manual of the American Psychological Association. 6th ed. Washington (DC): American Psychological Association; 2010.
Book, edited	Reference list	Baluka F, Mancuso S, Volkmann D, editors. Communication in plants: Neuronal aspects of plant life. Berlin: Springer-Verlag; 2006.
Chapter in edited book	Reference list	Kelley SO. Nanowires for biomolecular sensing. In: Vo-Dinh T, editor. Nanotechnology in biology and medicine: Methods, devices, and applications. Boca Raton (FL): CRC Press/Taylor & Francis; 2007. pp. 95–101.
Preprint	Reference list	Prgomet M, Georgiou A, Westbrook J. The impact of mobile handheld technology on hospital physicians' work practices and patient care: A systematic review. Preprint. J Am Med Inform Assoc [Internet]. 2009 [cited 2009 Oct 8]. Available from: http://www.jamia.org/cgi/reprint/M3215v1. doi:10.1197/jamia.M3215

Government document	Reference list	Marinopoulos SS, Dorman T, Ratanawongsa N, Wilson LM, Ashar BH, Magaziner JL, Miller RG, Thomas PA, Prokopowicz GP, Qayyum R, Bass EB. Effectiveness of continuing medical education. Rockville (MD): Agency for Healthcare Research and Quality; 2007. AHRQ Pub. No. 07-E006.
		[AHRQ] Agency for Healthcare Research and Quality. Testing for cytochrome P450 poly-morphisms in adults with non-psychotic depression treated with selective serotonin reuptake inhibitors (SSRIs) [Structured Abstract]. Rockville (MD): AHRQ; 2007 [cited 2010 May 5]. AHRQ Pub. No. 07-E002. Available from: http://www.ahrq.gov/clinic/tp/cyp450tp.htm
CD-ROM or DVD	Reference list	3D human anatomy: Regional edition [DVD-ROM]. London (England): Primal Pictures; 2009.
Database	Reference list	RCSB Protein Data Bank [Internet]. 2010 [cited 2010 May 5]. Available from: http://www.rcsb.org/pdb/home/home.do
		[NIH] National Institutes of Health, Office of Dietary Supplements. International Biblio-graphic Information on Dietary Supplements (IBIDS) Database [Internet]. 2010 [cited 2007 Feb. 23]. Available from: http://ods.od.nih.gov/Health_Information/IBIDS.aspx
Website or web page	Reference list	[CSE] Council of Science Editors. Citing the Internet: Formats for bibliographic citation [Internet]. Reston (VA): Council of Science Editors; [date unknown]. [cited 2010 May 5]. Available from: http://www.councilscienceeditors.org/publications/citing_internet.cfm
		[USDA] US Department of Agriculture, Agricultural Research Service. Home page [Internet]. Washington (DC): USDA; 2009. [cited 2009 Nov 8]. Available from: http://www.ars.usda.gov/main/main.htm

[NLM] National Library of Medicine. Bookshelf
[Internet]. [date unknown]. [cited 2010 May 5].
Available from: http://www.ncbi.nlm.nih.gov
/sites/entrez?db=Books

▸ Where this citation says [Internet], yours might
    say [monograph on Internet] or [database on
    Internet].

Although individual references (shown above) are the same for both
the citation-sequence and citation-name systems, their full reference lists
are compiled in different orders.

Order of items within reference lists:

- Citation-name system: alphabetical by author
- Citation-sequence system: order of first appearance in the text

To illustrate, let's take the opening sentence of an article and show how
each style would handle the citations and reference list.

CSE: CITATION-SEQUENCE SYSTEM (ILLUSTRATION OF REFERENCE LIST ORDER)

Opening
sentence

This research deals with the ABC transporter family and
builds on prior studies by Thacker et al.,[1] Sheps et al.,[2]
and Kerr.[3]

Reference
list (in order
of appearance
in text)

1. Thacker C, Sheps JA, Rose AM. Caenorhabditis elegans
   dpy-5 is a cuticle procollagen processed by a proprotein
   convertase. Cell Mol Life Sci. 2006;63:1193–1204.
2. Sheps JA, Ralph S, Zhao Z, Baillie DL, Ling V. The ABC
   transporter gene family of Caenorhabditis elegans
   has implications for the evolutionary dynamics of
   multidrug resistance in eukaryotes. Genome Biol.
   2004;5:R15.
3. Kerr ID. Sequence analysis of twin ATP binding cassette
   proteins involved in translational control, antibiotic
   resistance, and ribonuclease L inhibition. Biochem Biophys
   Res Commun. 2004;315:166–173.

▸ Thacker's article is listed first because it is the first one mentioned
    in the text.

CSE: CITATION-NAME SYSTEM (ILLUSTRATION OF REFERENCE LIST ORDER)

Opening sentence	This research deals with the ABC transporter family and builds on prior studies by Thacker et al.,[3] Sheps et al.,[2] and Kerr.[1]

Reference list (alphabetical)	1.	Kerr ID. Sequence analysis of twin ATP binding cassette proteins involved in translational control, antibiotic resistance, and ribonuclease L inhibition. Biochem Biophys Res Commun. 2004;315:166–173.
	2.	Sheps JA, Ralph S, Zhao Z, Baillie DL, Ling V. The ABC transporter gene family of Caenorhabditis elegans has implications for the evolutionary dynamics of multidrug resistance in eukaryotes. Genome Biol. 2004;5:R15.
	3.	Thacker C, Sheps JA, Rose AM. Caenorhabditis elegans dpy-5 is a cuticle procollagen processed by a proprotein convertase. Cell Mol Life Sci. 2006;63:1193–1204.

▸ Thacker's article is listed last because it is last alphabetically.

The two systems, citation-sequence and citation-name, present *each item* in the reference list the same way. What's different are (1) the *order* of items in the reference list and (2) their *citation numbers* in the text.

There's one more item you may wish to include in your citations: the PMID number. All medical articles have this electronic tag, which identifies them within the comprehensive PubMed database. The PMID appears as the last item in the citation and is *not* followed by a period:

Kerr ID. Sequence analysis of twin ATP binding cassette proteins involved in translational control, antibiotic resistance, and ribonuclease L inhibition. Biochem Biophys Res Commun [Internet]. 2004 [cited 2007 Feb 12]; 315:166–173. PMID: 15013441

The PubMed database, covering more than four thousand biomedical journals, was developed at the National Library of Medicine and is available online at http://www.ncbi.nlm.nih.gov/pubmed/.

Detailed information about CSE citations for the sciences can be found in

- *Scientific Style and Format: The CSE Manual for Authors, Editors, and Publishers*, 7th ed. (Reston, VA: Council of Science Editors, 2006).

8 AMA CITATIONS FOR THE BIOMEDICAL SCIENCES, MEDICINE, NURSING, AND DENTISTRY

AMA citations are used in biomedical research, medicine, nursing, dentistry, and some related fields of biology. They are based on the *AMA Manual of Style: A Guide for Authors and Editors*, 10th ed. (Oxford: Oxford University Press, 2007).

Citations are numbered (1), (2), (3), in the order they appear in the text. Full references appear at the end of the paper—in the same order. For coauthored books and articles, you should list up to six authors. If there are more, list only the first three, followed by "et al." Rather than using the authors' first names, use their initials (without periods) and do not put spaces between the initials: Lipson CH. Abbreviate the titles of journals. Journal titles along with their standard abbreviations can be found in the PubMed journals database available at http://www.ncbi.nlm.nih .gov/journals.

AMA CITATIONS

Journal article	Van Gijn J, Kerr RS, Rinkel GJE. Subarachnoid haemorrhage. *Lancet.* 2007;369(9558):306–318.
	Sehgal S, Drazner MH. Left ventricular geometry: does shape matter? *Am Heart J.* 2007;153(2):153–155.

▸ AMA uses sentence style for journals titles and does *not* capitalize the first letter of a subtitle.

Drinka PJ, Krause PF, Nest LJ, Goodman BM. Determinants of vitamin D levels in nursing home residents. *J Am Med Dir Assoc.* 2007;8(2):76–79.

▸ Journal titles are abbreviated without periods. (There's a period after "*Assoc.*" only to separate the journal title from the information about date, volume and issue, and pagination.)

▸ Name up to six authors in articles or books. If there are more, name the first three, then use "et al." This article, for example, has thirteen listed authors:

Morton N, Maniatis N, Weihua Z, et al. Genome scanning by composite likelihood. *Am J Hum Genet.* 2007;80(1):19–28.

▸ For more than one group of authors—common in medical papers—separate them by a semicolon. Terms such as "for" or "and" are optional:

Singh AK, Szczech L, Tang KL, et al; for CHOIR Investigators. Correction of anemia with epoetin alfa in chronic kidney disease. *N Engl J Med.* 2006;355(20):2085–2098.

▸ AMA's use of period-free abbreviations extends to many terms, including "et al"—in which "et" is a word and "al" is an abbreviation. (Most publications would write it "et al."—with a period.)

Journal article, online	Jia X, Wei M, Fu X, et al. Intensive cholesterol-lowering therapy improves large artery elasticity in acute myocardial infarction patients. *Heart Vessels.* 2009;24(5):340–346. doi:10.1007 /s00380-008-1132-z.

▸ Digital Object Identifiers (DOIs) are available for many journal articles—in fact, it's becoming hard to find an extant medical journal that doesn't assign them. The AMA prefers DOIs to URLs. When you cite a DOI, you do not have to list a URL or an access date. An access date is required, however, if you list a URL:

Moriguchi A, Nakagami H, Kotani N, Higaki J, Ogihara T. Contribution of cardiovascular hypersensitivity to orthostatic hypertension and the extreme dipper phenomenon. *Hypertens Res.* 2000;23(2):119–123. http://www.journalarchive.jst.go.jp /jnlpdf.php?cdjournal=hypres1992&cdvol=23&noissue=2 &startpage=119&lang=en&from=jnltoc. Accessed May 5, 2010.

▸ For citations of journal articles, ALA recommends copying the URL from the address bar in your browser rather than citing a home page—apparently without regard for length.

Abstract of article	Erkut S, Uckan S. Alveolar distraction osteogenesis and implant placement in a severely resorbed maxilla: a clinical report [abstract]. *J Prosthet Dent.* 2006;95(5):340–343.

Erkut S, Uckan S. Alveolar distraction osteogenesis and implant placement in a severely resorbed maxilla: a clinical report [abstract taken from *Dent Abstr.* 2007;52(1):17–19]. *J Prosthet Dent.* 2006;95(5):340–343.

▸ The upper reference is to the abstract, as published in the article itself. The lower reference is to the abstract, published in a different journal.

Preprint or unpublished paper	Prgomet M, Georgiou A, Westbrook J. The impact of mobile handheld technology on hospital physicians' work practices and patient care: a systematic review [published online ahead of print August 28, 2009]. *J Am Med Inform Assoc.* doi:10.1197 /jamia.M3215. ▸ Once the journal has been published, information about issue and pagination should be added to the citation. Hamilton P. Selective laser retinal pigment epithelium treatment for diabetic macular edema. Paper presented at: Retina Subspecialty Day, Annual Meeting of the American Academy of Ophthalmology; November 10, 2007; New Orleans, LA.
Published letter, comment, or editorial	Guazzi M, Reina G. Regarding article, Aspirin use and outcomes in a community-based cohort of 7352 patients discharged after first hospitalization for heart failure [letter]. *Circulation.* 2007;115(4):e54. doi:10.1161/CIRCULATIONAHA.106.646182. Simon DI, Pompili VJ. Far-fetched benefit of inflammation [editorial]. *Circulation.* 2007;115(5):548–549.
Book, one author	O'Grady E. *A Nurse's Guide to Caring for Cardiac Intervention Patients.* Chichester, England: John Wiley & Sons; 2007. ▸ Book titles use caps for main words. Articles use caps only for the first word in the article title. Wiggins CE. *A Concise Guide to Orthopaedic and Musculoskeletal Impairment Ratings.* Philadelphia, PA: Lippincott Williams & Wilkins; 2007. Hands L. *Vascular Surgery.* New York, NY: Oxford; 2007. ▸ Note that states are included even after well-known cities.
Book, multiple authors	Hill, J, Courtenay, M. *Prescribing in Diabetes.* Cambridge, England: Cambridge University Press; 2008.
Book, multiple editions	Snell RS. *Clinical Anatomy by Regions.* 8th ed. Philadelphia, PA: Lippincott Williams & Wilkins; 2007. Higgins CB, de Roos A, eds. *MRI and CT of the Cardiovascular System.* 2nd ed. Philadelphia, PA: Lippincott Williams & Wilkins; 2006.

Mazze R, Strock ES, Simonson GD, Bergenstal RM. *Staged Diabetes Management*. 2nd rev ed. Hoboken, NJ: John Wiley & Sons; 2007.

▸ The edition number appears between the book's title and the place of publication.

▸ For an unnumbered revised edition, use "Rev ed" (followed by a period) in place of the specific edition.

Book, multiple volumes	Chorghade MS, ed. *Drug Discovery and Development*. 2 vols. Hoboken, NJ: John Wiley & Sons; 2007. ▸ To cite only the second volume: Chorghade MS, ed. *Drug Discovery and Development*. Vol 2. Hoboken, NJ: John Wiley & Sons; 2007. ▸ The abbreviation for "volume" does not have a period. AMA eliminates periods after abbreviations. ▸ To cite the second volume by name, begin with the author (or editor) of that volume, plus its title and publication date, followed by the series name and the volume within the series. You do not need to include the editor of the series, even if it's different from the editor of the volume. Chorghade MS, ed. *Drug Development*. Hoboken, NJ: John Wiley & Sons; 2007. *Drug Discovery and Development*; vol 2.
Book, multiple editions, no author	*Dorland's Illustrated Medical Dictionary*. 31st ed. Philadelphia, PA: Saunders; 2007. *Nursing 2009 Drug Handbook*. 29th ed. Philadelphia, PA: Lippincott Williams & Wilkins; 2008.
Reference book	Vandersall D. *Concise Encyclopedia of Periodontology*. Ames, IA: Blackwell; 2007. Lewis RJ Sr. *Hawley's Condensed Chemical Dictionary*. 15th ed. New York, NY: John Wiley & Sons; 2007. Federative International Committee on Anatomical Terminology (FICAT). *Terminologia Histologica: International Terms for Human Cytology and Histology*. Philadelphia, PA: Lippincott Williams & Wilkins; 2007. Fuster V, O'Rourke RA, Walsh, RA, et al, eds. *Hurst's The Heart*. 12th ed. New York, NY: McGraw-Hill; 2008.

Reference online and CD	*Medical Dictionary (Medline)*. http://www.nlm.nih.gov/medlineplus/mplusdictionary.html. Accessed May 5, 2010.
	Walsh, RA, Simon, DI, Hoit BD, Fang JC, Costa M. *Hurst's The Heart*. 12th ed. New York, NY: McGraw-Hill; 2008. http://www.accessmedicine.com/resourceTOC.aspx?resourceID=5. Accessed May 5, 2010.
	Dorland's Online Dictionary. http://www.dorlands.com/wsearch.jsp. Accessed May 5, 2010.
	Lewis RJ Sr. *Hawley's Condensed Chemical Dictionary* [CD-ROM]. 15th ed. New York, NY: John Wiley & Sons; 2007.
Book, edited	Oppenheimer SJ ed. *Neural Tube Defects*. New York, NY: Informa Healthcare USA; 2007.
	Gravlee GP, Davis RF, Stammers AH, Ungerleider RM, eds. *Cardiopulmonary Bypass Principles and Practice*. 3rd ed. Philadelphia, PA: Lippincott Williams & Wilkins; 2007.
Chapter in edited book	Matthias Föhn M, Bannasch H. Artificial skin. In: Hauser H, Fussenegger M, ed. *Tissue Engineering*. 2nd ed. Totowa, NJ: Humana Press; 2007:732–739.
	Rizk NJ. Parallel and computational approaches to evolutionary biology. In: Zomaya AY, ed. *Parallel Computing for Bioinformatics and Computational Biology: Models, Enabling Technologies, and Case Studies*. Hoboken, NJ: John Wiley & Sons; 2006:3–28.
Government document, hard copy or online	Agency for Healthcare Research and Quality (AHRQ). Testing for cytochrome P450 polymorphisms in adults with non-psychotic depression treated with selective serotonin reuptake inhibitors (SSRIs) [structured abstract]. January 2007. AHRQ, Rockville, MD. http://www.ahrq.gov/clinic/tp/cyp450tp.htm. Accessed May 5, 2010.
	Marinopoulos SS, Dorman T, Ratanawongsa N, et al. Effectiveness of continuing medical education. AHRQ Pub No 07-E006. Rockville, MD: Agency for Healthcare Research and Quality; 2007.

Medicare Advantage cost plans and demonstrations: landscape of plan options in Mississippi 2007. Washington, DC: US Dept of Health and Human Services, date unknown. http://www.medicare.gov/medicarereform/mapdpdocs2007 /MAPDLandscapeMS07.pdf. Accessed May 5, 2010.

Personal communications	▸ Using AMA style, your reference list cannot include personal communications such as letters, e-mails, private discussions, or informal talks. Instead, cite those in the text.

CD-ROM or DVD	National Library of Medicine. *Changing the Face of Medicine* [DVD]. Washington, DC: Friends of the National Library of Medicine; 2004.
	3D Human Anatomy [DVD-ROM]. London, England: Primal Pictures; 2009.

Database	RCSB Protein Data Bank. http://www.rcsb.org/pdb/home/home .do. Accessed May 5, 2010.
	National Institutes of Health. Office of Dietary Supplements. International Bibliographic Information on Dietary Supplements (IBIDS) Database. http://ods.od.nih.gov/Health_Information /IBIDS.aspx. Accessed May 5, 2010.
	National Center for Health Statistics. Summary health statistics for the U.S. population: national health interview survey, 2008.
	Vital Health Stat 10 (243). DHHS Pub No 2010–1571. Hyattsville, MD: National Center for Health Statistics (US Dept of Health and Human Services); 2009.

Website or web page	Interim guidance for 2009 H1N1 flu (swine flu): taking care of a sick person in your home. Centers for Disease Control and Prevention. http://www.cdc.gov/H1N1flu/guidance_homecare .htm. Published October 23, 2009. Accessed November 9, 2009.
	Hellinger FJ, Encinosa WE. Impact of state laws limiting malpractice awards on geographic distribution of physicians. US Department of Health and Human Services, Agency for Healthcare Research and Quality. http://www.ahrq.gov/ RESEARCH/tortcaps/tortcaps.htm. Published July 3, 2003. Accessed May 5, 2010.

To illustrate how these citations appear in the text, let's take the opening sentence of an article.

AMA (ILLUSTRATION OF REFERENCE LIST ORDER)

Opening sentence	This research deals with the ABC transporter family and builds on prior studies by Thacker et al,[1] Sheps et al,[2] and Kerr.[3]

Reference list (in order of appearance in text)	1.	Thacker C, Sheps JA, Rose AM. *Caenorhabditis elegans dpy-5* is a cuticle procollagen processed by a proprotein convertase. *Cell Mol Life Sci.* 2006;63(10):1193–1204.
	2.	Sheps JA, Ralph S, Zhao Z, Baillie DL, Ling V. The ABC transporter gene family of *Caenorhabditis elegans* has implications for the evolutionary dynamics of multidrug resistance in eukaryotes. *Genome Biol.* 2004;5(3):R15.
	3.	Kerr ID. Sequence analysis of twin ATP binding cassette proteins involved in translational control, antibiotic resistance, and ribonuclease L inhibition. *Biochem Biophys Res Commun.* 2004;315(1):166–173.

▸ Thacker's article is listed first because it is the first one mentioned in the text. Notice that "et al" does not include a period when it is used in sentences, according to AMA style.

Finally, all medical articles have an electronic identification number, known as a PMID. You are not required to include it, but it often helps your readers. It will help you, too, if you need to return to the article. If you include a PMID, you do not need to include a DOI or URL. The PMID appears as the last item in the citation and is followed by a period:

Yeates TO. Protein structure: evolutionary bridges to new folds. *Curr Biol.* 2007;17(2):R48–50. PMID: 17240325.

The PMID identifies the document within the PubMed database, which includes virtually all biomedical journals. This database was developed at the National Library of Medicine, and it is available online at http://www.ncbi.nlm.nih.gov/pubmed/.

9 ACS CITATIONS FOR CHEMISTRY

The American Chemical Society (ACS) has its own style guide, which gives you a choice of citation formats:

- In-text citations with name and year, similar to APA or CSE. The reference list is alphabetized and appears at the end of the paper.
- Numbered citations, with a reference list at the end of the paper. End references are numbered in the order they appear in the text. These numbered citations, as they appear in the text itself, are either
  - superscript, such as[23], or
  - parentheses with the number in italics, such as (*23*).

Each format is used by scores of chemistry journals. Your lab, instructor, or journal may prefer one over the other. Whichever one you choose, use it consistently throughout each paper.

Fortunately, you collect the same information for either format. In fact, the items in the reference list are presented exactly the same way, whether the list is numbered or alphabetized.

- The author's last name appears first, followed by a comma and then initials (instead of given names), such as Fenn, J. B. Initials are followed by periods.
- Instead of "page," the reference list uses "p" and "pp" without periods.
- The reference list uses hanging indents. That is, the first line of each reference is full length; all subsequent lines are indented.
- For books
  - Include the title and italicize it. That's true for edited books, too.
  - Put the publisher's name before the location, as in CRC Press: Boca Raton, FL.
  - Include the year of publication, using normal typeface, such as Wiley-Interscience: New York, 2004.
  - Show pagination in books by using "pp"—for example: CRC Press: Boca Raton, FL, 2004; pp 507–515.
  - For edited books, you may include (or omit) the titles of specific chapters; just be consistent.

- For journals
  - Include the journal title, abbreviated and italicized, such as *J. Am. Chem. Soc.*
  - Include the year of publication in **boldface**, the volume number in italics, and the complete pagination of the article in normal type, such as *Org. Lett.* **2007**, *9*, 2609–2611.
  - Show pagination in articles *without* using "pp"—for example: *Chem. Eng. News.* **2007**, *85*, 31–34.
  - Include or omit the article's title, whichever you prefer. (Be consistent, of course.) Until recently, article titles were always omitted. Now the *ACS Style Guide* (3rd ed.) considers it "desirable" to include the title, both to indicate the subject matter and to help readers find it.

There is no explanation for these mysterious details. My guess: the chemists were overcome by fumes many years ago, and the odd results are now beloved traditions.

ACS (CHEMISTRY): REFERENCE LIST AND IN-TEXT CITATIONS

Journal article	Reference list	Luft, J.; Meleson, K.; Houk, K. Transition Structures of Diastereoselective 1,3-Dipolar Cycloadditions of Nitrile Oxides to Chiral Homoallylic Alcohols. *Org. Lett.* **2007**, *9*, 555–558.

▶ Or

Luft, J.; Meleson, K.; Houk, K. *Org. Lett.* **2007**, *9*, 555–558.

Xing, Y.; Lin, H.; Wang, F.; Lu, P. An Efficient D-A Dyad for Solvent Polarity Sensor. *Sens. Actuators, B* **2006**, *114*, 28–31.

▶ Or

Xing, Y.; Lin, H.; Wang, F.; Lu, P. *Sens. Actuators, B* **2006**, *114*, 28–31.

▶ Authors' names are separated by semicolons.

▶ Article title may be included or omitted. The *ACS Style Guide* (3rd ed.) recommends inclusion. Words in the article title are capitalized, as they would be in a book title.

▶ Year of publication is in boldface; volume number is italicized.

> ► Journal titles are italicized and abbreviated according to the *Chemical Abstracts Service Source Index* (CASSI).

	In-text	(Luft et al., 2007) (Xing et al., 2006)

Journal article, online	Reference list	Zaki, M.; Nirdosh, I.; Sedahmed, G. *Chem. Eng. J.* [Online] **2007**, *126*, 67–77.
	In-text	(Zaki et al., 2007)

Chemical abstract	Reference list	Taneda, A.; Shimizu, T.; Kawazoe, Y. *J. Phys.: Condens. Matter* **2001**, *13* (16), L305–312 (Eng.); *Chem. Abstr.* **2001**, *134*, 372018a.

> ► This article by Taneda et al. was published in a journal and referenced in *Chemical Abstracts*. This citation shows a reference to both the full article and the abstract. The abstract always comes second and is separated from the article by a semicolon.

Taneda, A.; Shimizu, T.; Kawazoe, Y. *Chem. Abstr.* **2001**, *134*, 372018a.

> ► Same article but shown only as mentioned in *Chemical Abstracts*. It is better to refer to the full published article than to the abstract, but that requires you actually examine the full article.

Chem. Abstr. **2001**, *134*, 372018a.

> ► This is the same article, referred to solely by its *Chemical Abstract* number. That number—*134*, 372018a—is the CAS accession number. The number *134* is the volume and 372018a is the abstract number in the print version of *Chemical Abstracts*. These numbers also work with the CAS databases that have recently taken the place of the printed *Abstracts*.

> ► In editions of *Chemical Abstracts* prior to 1967, abstracts did not carry unique numbers. Instead, they must be identified by column number and their position on the page. Abstract f, column 1167, can be cited as 1167*f* (or 1167*ᶠ*).

> ► It is usually better to include the authors, as in the previous references to Taneda et al.

| | In-text | (Taneda et al., 2001) |
| | | (*Chem. Abstr.*, 2001) |

Book, one author	Reference list	Tilley, R. *Crystals and Crystal Structures;* John Wiley & Sons: Chichester, U.K., 2006; pp 23–42.
		▸ Or: Chapter 3 instead of the pagination.
	In-text	(Tilley, 2006)

Book, multiple authors	Reference list	Williams, R. J. P.; Fraústo da Silva, J. J. R. *The Chemistry of Evolution: The Development of Our Ecosystem;* Elsevier: Amsterdam, 2006.
		▸ What if there are many authors? The *ACS Style Guide* says to name them all. It also notes that some chemistry journals list only the first ten, followed by a semicolon and "et al."
	In-text	(Williams and Fraústo da Silva, 2006)
		▸ Include up to two names for in-text citations. If there are three or more, use this form: (Williams et al., 2006)

Book, multiple editions	Reference list	McMurry, J.; Castellion, M. E.; Ballantine, D. S.; Hoeger, C. A.; Peterson, V. E. *Fundamentals of General, Organic, and Biological Chemistry*, 6th ed.; Prentice-Hall: Upper Saddle River, NJ, 2009.
		▸ For a revised edition, use "Rev. ed." instead of "6th ed."
	In-text	(McMurry et al., 2009)

Book multiple editions, no author	Reference list	*Reagent Chemicals: Specifications and Procedures*, 10th ed.; American Chemical Society: Washington, DC, 2005.
		McGraw-Hill Encyclopedia of Science and Technology, 10th ed.; McGraw-Hill: New York, 2009; 20 vols.
	In-text	(*Reagent Chemicals*, 2005).
		(*McGraw-Hill*, 2009)

▶ To cite a particular volume:
(*McGraw-Hill*, Vol. 6, 2002)

Book, multivolume	Reference list	*The Encyclopedia of Mass Spectrometry*; Gross, M. L., Caprioli, R., Eds.; Elsevier Science: Oxford, 2007; Vol. 6. *Hyphenated Methods*; Niessen, W., Ed. Vol. 8. In *The Encyclopedia of Mass Spectrometry*; Gross, M. L., Caprioli, R., Eds.; Elsevier Science: Oxford, 2007.
	In-text	(Gross and Caprioli, Vol. 6, 2007) (Niessen, Vol. 8, 2007)
Book, edited	Reference list	*Polyketides: Biosynthesis, Biological Activity, and Genetic Engineering*; Rimando, A. M., Baerson, S. R., Eds.; American Chemical Society: Washington, DC, 2007.
	In-text	(Rimando and Baerson, 2007) ▶ For in-text references, editors' names are treated the same as authors'.
Chapter in edited book	Reference list	Lavine, B. K., et al. In *Chemometrics and Chemoinformatics*; Lavine, B. K., Ed.; American Chemical Society: Washington, DC, 2005; pp 127–143. ▶ Or Lavine, B. K.; Davidson, C. E.; Breneman, C.; Katt, W. In *Chemometrics and Chemoinformatics*; Lavine, B. K., Ed.; American Chemical Society: Washington, DC, 2005; pp 127–143. ▶ You may include or omit the chapter title (which would be styled like the title of a journal article); just be consistent.
	In-text	(Lavine et al., 2005) ▶ Normally use only one or two names for in-text citations. Occasionally, though, you will find top chemistry journals citing more authors, such as: (Lavine, Davidson, Breneman, and Katt, 2005)

Conference paper	Reference list	Monti, M.; Cataletto, B. Molecular Characterization and Morphological Variability of Seven Strains of the Dinoflagellate *Prorocentrum Minimum* PO.01-07. Presented at the 12th International Conference on Harmful Algae, Copenhagen, Denmark, September 2006; Poster.
	In-text	(Monti and Cataletto, 2006)
Reference work or encyclopedia	Reference list	Vaidya, R.; López, G.; Lopez, J. A. Nanotechnology (Molecular). *Van Nostrand's Encyclopedia of Chemistry* [Online]; John Wiley & Sons: Hoboken, NJ, 2005. http://www3.interscience.wiley .com/cgi-bin/mrwhome/110498369/HOME (accessed May 5, 2010).
	In-text	(Vaidya et al., 2005)
Government document	Reference list	U.S. Consumer Product Safety Commission. *School Chemistry Laboratory Safety Guide (October 2006)*; DHHS (NIOSH) Publication No. 2007–107; National Institute for Occupational Safety and Health: Cincinnati, OH, 2007. National Emission Standards for Hazardous Air Pollutants for Source Categories from Oil and Natural Gas Production Facilities. *Fed. Regist.* 2007, *72* (1), 26–43. ▸ The *Federal Register* is treated like a journal.
	In-text	(U.S. Consumer Product Safety Commission, 2007) (National Emission Standards, 2007)
Patent	Reference list	Lieber, C. M., et al. Methods of Forming Nanoscopic Wire-Based Devices and Arrays. U.S. Patent 7,172,953 B2, 2007. ▸ It is also acceptable to omit the name of the patent.
	In-text	(Lieber et al., 2007)

CD-ROM or DVD	Reference list	Luceigh, B. A. *Chem TV: Organic Chemistry* 3.0 [CD-ROM]; Jones and Bartlett: Sudbury, MA, 2004. Lewis, R. J., Sr. *Hawley's Condensed Chemical Dictionary*, 15th ed. [CD-ROM]; John Wiley & Sons: New York, 2007. Lide, D. R. *Handbook of Chemistry and Physics on CD-ROM Version 2007*, 8th ed. [CD-ROM]; CRC Press/Taylor & Francis: Boca Raton, FL, 2006.
	In-text	(Luceigh, 2004) (Lewis, 2007) (Lide, 2006)
Internet	Reference list	Biochemical Periodic Tables. http://umbbd .msi.umn.edu/periodic/links.html (accessed May 5, 2010). ▸ If the page has an author, his name and initial appear before the title of the page: Oxtoby, J. Biochemical Periodic Tables. http:// . . .
	In-text	(Biochemical Periodic Tables, 2010) ▸ If no date of publication is included with a document on a website, use the access date for the in-text citation.

Detailed information on ACS citations is available in

• Anne M. Coghill and Lorrin R. Garson, eds., *The ACS Style Guide: Effective Communication of Scientific Information,* 3rd ed. (Washington, DC: American Chemical Society, 2006).

10 PHYSICS, ASTROPHYSICS, AND ASTRONOMY CITATIONS

AIP CITATIONS IN PHYSICS

Physics citations are based on the *AIP Style Manual*, 4th ed. (New York: American Institute of Physics, 1990) and the more recent *AIP Physics Desk Reference*, 3rd ed. (2003).[1] Most physics journals use numbered citations in the text and the reference list. Items appear in the numbered reference list in the order they appear in the text.

The citations may be numbered either in superscript or brackets, that is, as [99] or [99]. The *AIP Style Manual* uses superscripts, as do AIP's official journals, such as *Chaos* and *Low Temperature Physics*. On the other hand, the organization's own *AIP Physics Desk Reference* uses brackets, as do journals from the American Physical Society (APS), such as *Physical Review E*. Either approach is fine. Just be sure you use the same style for the text and reference list. (A few physics journals use the author-year style instead. It has an alphabetized reference list with hanging indents.)

Whichever format is used, individual items in the reference list look the same, at least for articles and preprints (which are the way researchers communicate). References are brief: Authors' names as they appear on the title page of the work (M. Shochet and S. Nagel), abbreviated journal title, **boldface number for the journal volume**, first page number of the article, and, finally, the year in parentheses.

AIP (PHYSICS): REFERENCE LIST

Journal article

[1] O. Budriga and V. Florescu, Euro. Phys. J. D **41**, 205 (2007).

[2] A. N. Khorramian, S. Atashbar Tehrani, and A. Mirjalili, Nucl. Phys. B **164** (Proc. Suppl.) 34 (2007).

▸ The article's title is always omitted. Journal titles are abbreviated and not italicized.

---

1. E. Richard Cohen, David R. Lide, and George L. Trigg, eds., *AIP Physics Desk Reference*, 3rd ed. (New York: Springer-Verlag, 2003).

▸ The publication volume (or issue number) and series are in boldface. For example, if a reference is to an article in *Physical Letters B*, issue number 466, page 415, then it appears as Phys. Lett. B **466**, 415 (1999).

Journal article, online	[#] Tuson Park and J. D. Thompson, New J. Phys. **11**, 055062 (2009). <http://stacks.iop.org/1367-2630/11/055062>. ▸ This is an online-only journal; instead of page numbers, it assigns article numbers (in the case of the Park and Thompson article, 055062). ▸ The citation may also include a Digital Object Identifier (DOI) after the URL. The DOI is a unique identifier assigned to most STM journal articles. For the Park and Thompson article, doi:10.1088/1367-2630/11/5/055062.
Preprint	[#] Anna Hasenfratz, preprint, arXiv:0911.0646v1 [hep-lat] (2009). <http://arxiv.org/PS_cache/arxiv/pdf/0911/0911.0646v1.pdf>. [#] J. Messud, M. Bender, E. Suraud, preprint, arXiv:0904.0162v2 [nucl-th] (2009). <http://arxiv.org/PS_cache/arxiv/pdf/0904/0904.0162v2.pdf>. To be published in Phys. Rev. C. [#] A. J. M. Medved, preprint, arXiv:hep-th/0301010v2 (2003). <http://arxiv.org/PS_cache/hep-th/pdf/0301/0301010v2.pdf>. Published in High Energy Phys. **5**, 008 (2003). <http://www.iop.org/EJ/abstract/1126-6708/2003/05/008/>. doi:10.1088/1126-6708/2003/05/008. ▸ hep-lat = Heidelberg High Energy Physics (HEP) Preprint Service, e-prints on lattices; nucl-th = nuclear theory; hep-th = e-prints on theoretical physics.
Book, one author	[#] Robert M. White, *Quantum Theory of Magnetism: Magnetic Properties of Materials* (Springer, Berlin, 2007).
Book, multiple authors	[#] Dante Gatteschi, Roberta Sessoli, and Jacques Villain, *Molecular Nanomagnets* (Oxford University Press, Oxford, 2006). ▸ The *AIP Style Manual* says to list up to three authors. If there are more authors, name only the first and add "*et al.*" in italics. Example: Dante Gatteschi *et al.*, *Molecular Nanomagnets* . . .

Book, multiple editions	[#] A. F. J. Levi, *Applied Quantum Mechanics*, 2nd ed. (Cambridge University Press, New York, 2006).
Book, multivolume	[#] J.-P. Françoise, G. L. Naber, and T. S. Tsun, editors, *Encyclopedia of Mathematical Physics*, 5 vols. (Academic Press/Elsevier, San Diego, CA, 2006).
Book, edited	[#] Zhigang Li and Hong Meng, editors, *Organic Light-Emitting Materials and Devices* (CRC Press/Taylor & Francis, Boca Raton, FL, 2007).
Chapter in book	[#] Heinz Georg Schuster, in *Collective Dynamics of Nonlinear and Disordered Systems*, edited by G. Radons, W. Just, and P. Häussler (Springer, Berlin, 2005).
Database	[#] National Institutes of Standards and Technology, Physics Laboratory, Physical Reference Data. <http://physics.nist.gov/PhysRefData/>.

CITATIONS IN ASTROPHYSICS AND ASTRONOMY

Astronomy and astrophysics don't use the AIP/physics citation style or, for that matter, any single format. But most leading journals are fairly similar. They generally use (author-year) citations in the text, followed by an alphabetical reference list. The reference list follows some fairly common rules. It generally

- uses hanging indents
- contains no bold or italics
- uses authors' initials rather than their first names
- joins coauthors' names with an ampersand "&"
- puts the publication date immediately after the author's name (with no comma between the name and date)
- omits the titles of articles
- includes titles for books and gives publisher information
- abbreviates journal names, often reducing them to a couple of initials

- lists only the first page of an article
- ends references without a period

Because there's no published style manual for astronomy and astrophysics, citation formats vary. I've standardized them, based on the most common forms in the leading journals. Here are some illustrations, based on *Astronomy and Astrophysics* and the *Astrophysical Journal*, with a little tweaking for consistency.

ASTRONOMY AND ASTROPHYSICS REFERENCE LISTS

Journal article	Baugh, C. M. 2006, Rept. Prog. Phys., 69, 3101
	Li, D., et al. 2007, ApJ, 655, 351
	Stroman, T., Pohl, M., & Niemiec, J. 2009, ApJ, 706, 38
	Fechner, C., & Reimers, D. 2007, A&A, 461, 847

Journal article, several by same authors	Panaitescu, A. 2005a, MNRAS, 363, 1409
	Panaitescu, A. 2005b, MNRAS, 362, 921
	Razzaque, S., & Mészáros, P. 2006a, ApJ, 650, 998
	Razzaque, S., & Mészáros, P. 2006b, JCAP, 06, 006
	Pe'er, A., & Wijers, R. A. M. J. 2006, ApJ, 643, 1036
	Pe'er, A., & Zhang, B. 2006, ApJ, 653, 454

> ▸ The two articles by Panaitescu are listed as 2005a and 2005b because they have the same author.
> ▸ The two articles by Razzaque & Mészáros are listed as 2006a and 2006b because they have the same coauthors.
> ▸ The two articles by Pe'er are *not* listed as 2006a and 2006b because they do not have identical coauthors.

Journal article, online	Khomenko, E., & Collados, M. 2009, A&A 506, L5, doi:10.1051 /0004-6361/200913030

> ▸ *All* astronomy, astrophysics, and physics articles are online and available through standard scientific databases. Adding the Digital Object Identifier or other search information may help your readers find them more easily.

Preprint	Law, C. J. 2009, ApJ, in press, arXiv:0911.2061v1 [astro-ph.GA]
	Zaballa, I., & Sasaki, M. 2009, preprint, arXiv:0911.2069v1 [astro-ph.CO]

Book, one author	Osterbrock, D. E. 2006, Astrophysics of Gaseous Nebulae and Active Galactic Nuclei (Sausalito, CA: University Science Books) Harwit, M. 2006, Astrophysical Concepts (New York: Springer Science)
Book, multiple authors	Cassen, P., Guillot, T., & Quirrenbach, A. 2006, Extrasolar Planets (New York: Springer)
Chapter in edited book	Franceschini, A. 2006, in Joint Evolution of Black Holes and Galaxies, ed. M. Colpi, V. Gorini, F. Haardt, & U. Moschella (Boca Raton, FL: CRC Press/Taylor & Francis), 63
Book in a series	Stefl, S., Owocki, S. P., & Okazaki, A. T., eds., 2006, Active Ob-Stars: Laboratories for Stellar and Circumstellar Physics (San Francisco: ASP), ASP Conf. Ser. 361
Chapter in a book in a series	Daly, P. N. 2006, in Astronomical Data Analysis Software Systems XV, ed. C. Gabriel, C. Arviset, D. Ponz, & E. Solano (San Francisco: ASP), ASP Conf. Ser. 351, 4
Unpublished paper or dissertation	Sedrakian, A. 2007 arXiv:astro-ph/0701017v2, from lectures available at http://theor.jinr.ru/~dm2006/talks.html Egan, M. P., Price, S. D., Moshir, M. M., et al. 1999, Air Force Research Lab. Tech. Rep. no. AFRL-VS. T. R. 1999-1522 Fiore, F., Guainazzi, M., & Grandi, P. 1999, Cookbook for BeppoSAX NFI Spectral Analysis, available from ftp://ftp.asdc.asi.it/sax/doc/software_docs/saxabc_v1.2.ps.gz Lee, J. 2006, Ph.D. Diss., University of Arizona
Internet	SkyView, the Internet's Virtual Telescope <http://skyview.gsfc.nasa.gov/>

Researchers in the physical sciences often cite unpublished research, usually conference papers or work-in-progress that will be published later. Known as preprints (or e-prints), these papers are at the cutting edge of the field and are collected in electronic document archives. Besides collections at major research institutions, there's a huge collection at arXiv.org (http://arxiv.org/), with mirror sites around the world. Papers are readily accessible and easy to download. What's hard—unless you are on the cutting edge of physics—is actually understanding their content!

Preprints in the arXiv collection are classified by field (physics, astrophysics, mathematics, quantitative biology, and so forth) and, within each field, by major subfields. Papers are submitted to the subfield archives and are numbered by their date of arrival. As with journal articles, the titles of preprints are omitted from citations. Here are some examples:

> Ángeles Pérez-García, M. 2009, preprint, arXiv:0911.0378v1
> [nucl-th] <http://arxiv.org/PS_cache/arxiv/pdf/0911/0911
> .0378v1.pdf>
> Zasche, P., 2009, preprint, arXiv:0911.2079v1 [astro-ph.SR]

or

> Zasche, P., 2009, preprint (arXiv:0911.2079v1 [astro-ph.SR])

The classification system is as simple as the papers are complex. Take the Zasche paper. It's in the astrophysics archive (astro-ph), under the subject category solar and stellar astrophysics (SR), was submitted in 2009 (09), in November (11), and is version 1 of the 2079th paper submitted in its category that month. Hence, 0911.2079v1 [astro-ph.SR].

For the Ángeles Pérez-García article, I included the URL for the PDF version of the article, but that's not essential. Professionals in the field know where to find arXiv preprints, either at the main archive or mirror sites. It's sufficient to list the ID: arXiv:0911.0378v1 [nucl-th].

Preprints like these should be cited and included in your reference list, just like journal articles. Unpublished does not mean uncited.

11 MATHEMATICS, COMPUTER SCIENCE, AND ENGINEERING CITATIONS

MATHEMATICS AND COMPUTER SCIENCE

Papers in mathematics and computer science use one of two citation styles. The first places an alphabetical reference list at the end of the paper. References in the text are given by bracketed numbers. The first reference might be [23], referring to the twenty-third item in the alphabetical list. The last reference in the article might be [2]. Specific pages are rarely mentioned, but if you need to, use this form: [23, p. 14]. Please use the set of positive integers.

A second system, based on the *Bulletin of the American Mathematical Society,* is often used by advanced mathematicians for publishable research. It, too, has an alphabetical reference list (a slightly different one), but what's unusual are the text references. Instead of bracketed numbers, this style uses abbreviations, based on the author's last name and date of publication. So an article by Hirano and Porter, published in *Econometrica,* volume 77 (2009), would be cited in the text as something like [HiPo09] or perhaps [HP09] or maybe just [HP]. It's your choice. This abbreviation also appears in the reference list, identifying the entry for Hirano and Porter's article. In the second table below, I show how to use this AMS *Bulletin* system.

Most books and articles are classified by subfield and uniquely identified in the Mathematical Reviews (MR) Database. Whichever citation system you use, you can include this MR number as the last item in each reference, after the date or page numbers. The MR Database is searchable through the American Mathematical Society's website at http://www.ams.org/mr-database.

If the article you are citing is available online, perhaps at the author's website, mention the URL just before the MR number. If there is no MR number, the URL appears last.

In the following tables, I show standard mathematical citation forms. Many math journals don't stick to one format. Some use numerical citations for one article and AMS *Bulletin* style for the next. To add to the fun, they'll use the same style differently in different articles. One might list the author as R. Zimmer. The very next article (using the same style) lists the author as Zimmer, R. If I kept looking, I'd probably find one that calls him Bob Zimmer. One article puts the publication date in parentheses; the next one doesn't. In one, the reference list uses italics for every article title and regular type for journal names. The next one does exactly the opposite. Some use boldface for journal numbers, and others don't. Frankly, I don't think any of this matters very much, as long as you are consistent and your professor or publisher is okay with it.

In the tables below, I've swept away these variations and idiosyncrasies. The tables use consistent rules, based on recent editions of major journals in mathematics and computer science.

Article titles and book chapters are italicized. Capitalize only the first word, the first word after a colon, and all proper nouns:

F. Finster, N. Kamran, J. Smoller, and S.-T. Yau, *Linear waves in the Kerr geometry: A mathematical voyage to black hole physics*

Book titles are capitalized normally and italicized:

Nonlinear Optimization and Applications

Journal titles are abbreviated but not italicized:

Ann. of Math. Bull.
Amer. Math. Soc.
Geom. Topol.
Trans. Amer. Math. Soc.

A full list of journal abbreviations, compiled by the American Mathematical Society, is available at http://www.ams.org/msnhtml/serials.pdf.

Publications by the same author are listed in the order of publication, beginning with the earliest. Use three em dashes to repeat an author's name, but do so only if *all* the authors are the same. For example:

[32] S. Kihara, *On the rank of the elliptic curves with a rational point of order 4, II*, Proc. Japan Acad. Ser. A Math. Sci. 80 (2004), pp. 158–159.

[33] ———, *On the rank of elliptic curves with a rational point of order 6*, Proc. Japan Acad. Ser. A Math. Sci. 82 (2006), pp. 81–82.

[34] S. Kihara and M. Kenku, *Elliptic curves . . .*

MATHEMATICS: NUMBERED REFERENCE LIST (ALPHABETICAL ORDER)

Journal article	[1] B. Ahrenholz, J. Tölke, and M. Krafczyk, *Lattice-Boltzmann simulations in reconstructed parametrized porous media*, Int. J. Comput. Fluid Dyn. 20 (2006), pp. 369–377.

[2] I. D. Coope and C. J. Price, *Positive bases in numerical optimization*, Comput. Optim. Appl. 21 (2003), pp. 169–175.

[3] N. P. Strickland, *Gross-Hopkins duality*, Topology 39 (2000), pp. 1021–1033.

[4] ———, *Common subbundles and intersections of divisors*, Algebr. Geom. Topol. 2 (2002), pp. 1061–1118.

▸ Bracketed numbers go in the left margin. References are listed in alphabetical order, by author's name. For each author, the articles or books are listed in their order of publication, with the earliest ones first.

▸ If an author's name is repeated (and there are no new coauthors), then use three em dashes, followed by a comma. (Em dashes are simply long dashes, about the length of the letter "m." If for some reason, you can't find these em dashes, just use three hyphens.)

Journal article, online

[#] C. L. Fefferman, *Whitney's extension problem for C^m*, Ann. of Math. 164 (2006), pp. 313–359. Available at http://www.math.princeton.edu/facultypapers/Fefferman/.

[#] F. R. Harvey and H. B. Lawson Jr., *Duality of positive currents and plurisubharmonic functions in calibrated geometry*, Amer. J. Math. 131 (2009), pp. 1211–1239. Available at http://muse.jhu.edu/journals/american_journal_of_mathematics/summary/v131/131.5.harvey.html.

Preprint

[#] A. Böttcher and P. Dörfler, *Weighted Markov-type inequalities, norms of Volterra operators, and zeros of Bessel functions*, Technische Universität Chemnitz, Fakultät für Mathematik (Germany), preprint (2009).Available at http://www.mathematik.tu-chemnitz.de/preprint/quellen/2009/PREPRINT_01.pdf.

[#] S. Dasgupta and M. Greenberg, *L-invariants and Shimura curves*, preprint (2009), submitted for publication. Available at http://people.ucsc.edu/~sdasgup2/linvariants.pdf.

[#] C. Bakkari. *On Prüfer-like conditions*, preprint (2009). Available at http://arxiv.org/PS_cache/arxiv/pdf/0911/0911.2250v1.pdf.

[#] J.-R. Chazottes and M. Hochman, *On the zero-temperature limit of Gibbs states*, preprint (2009), to appear in Commun. Math. Phys. Available at arXiv:0907.0081v4 [math-ph].

[#] B. Chen, *The number of the Gabriel-Roiter measures admitting no direct predecessors over a wild quiver*, preprint (2009). Available at arXiv:0911.2249v1 [math.RT].

▶ In mathematics, as in physics, there's a large, easily accessible electronic archive of preprints available at arXiv. The math collection is at http://arxiv.org/archive/math. You can cite either the entire URL for a preprint, as the reference above for Bakkari does, or you can simply list the archival number and say it is available at arXiv, as the references for Chazottes and Hochman and for Chen do.

[#] X. Sun, *Singular structure of harmonic maps to trees*, preprint (2001), published as *Regularity of harmonic maps to trees*, Amer. J. Math. 125 (2003), pp. 737–771. MR1993740 (2004j:58014).

Other unpublished papers	[#] A. Iserles and S. P. Nørsett, *From high oscillation to rapid approximation II: Expansions in polyharmonic eigenfunctions*, DAMTP Tech. Rep. 2006/NA07. Department of Applied Mathematics and Theoretical Physics, University of Cambridge, Cambridge, UK, 2006. Available at http://www.damtp.cam.ac.uk/user/na/NA_papers/NA2006_07.pdf.
	[#] L. K. Kamenova, *Hyper-Kaehler fibrations and Hilbert schemes*, Ph.D. diss., MIT, 2006.
	[#] P. Rostalski, *Characterization and computation of real-radical ideals using semidefinite programming techniques*, IMA postdoc seminar, Minneapolis, MN, 2007.
Book, one author	[#] D. Eisenbud, *The Geometry of Syzygies: A Second Course in Commutative Algebra and Algebraic Geometry*, e-book, Springer, New York, 2005.
	[#] I. Ekeland, *The Best of All Possible Worlds: Mathematics and Destiny*, University of Chicago Press, Chicago, 2006.
	[#] A. Knapp, *Basic Algebra*, Birkhäuser, Boston, 2006.
	[#] M. A. Parthasarathy, *Practical Software Estimation: Function Point Methods for Insourced and Outsourced Projects*, Addison-Wesley Professional, Upper Saddle River, NJ, 2007.

Book, multiple authors	[#] T. Andreescu, O. Mushkarov, and L. Stoyanov, *Geometric Problems on Maxima and Minima*, Birkhäuser, Boston, 2006. ▸ If there are many authors, then name only the first and add "et al." Example: T. Andreescu et al., *Geometric Problems . . .*
Book, multiple editions	[#] H. Fulton, *The Ruby Way: Solutions and Techniques in Ruby Programming*, 2nd ed., Addison-Wesley Professional, Upper Saddle River, NJ, 2006. [#] B. Korte and J. Vygen, *Combinatorial Optimization: Theory and Algorithms*, 3rd ed., Springer-Verlag, Berlin, 2006. MR2171734 (2006d:90001).
Book, multivolume	[#] F. Dillen and L. C. A. Verstraelen (eds.), *Handbook of Differential Geometry*, vol. 2., Elsevier, Amsterdam, 2006. [#] D. Knuth, *The Art of Computer Programming*, 3rd ed., vol. 4, fasc. 3: *Generating All Combinations and Partitions*, Addison-Wesley Professional, Upper Saddle River, NJ, 2005. MR2251472. [#] G. W. Stewart, *Matrix Algorithms*. Vol. 2: *Eigensystems*, SIAM, Philadelphia, 2001.
Book, edited	[#] P. P. Kulish, N. Manojlovic, and H. Samtleben (eds.), *Infinite Dimensional Algebras and Quantum Integrable Systems*, Progress in Math., vol. 237, Birkhäuser, Boston, 2005.
Book, translated	[#] P. G. Darvas, *Symmetry*, trans. by D. R. Evans, Springer, New York, 2007.
Chapter in edited book	[#] J. Grabowski, *Local Lie algebra determines base manifold*, in *From Geometry to Quantum Mechanics: In Honor of Hideki Omori*, Progress in Math., vol. 252, Y. Maeda, P. Michor, T. Ochiai, and A. Yoshioka, eds., Birkhäuser, Boston, 2007, pp. 27–47. ▸ Notice that the chapter is capitalized like a sentence (i.e., only the first word and, in this case "Lie," which is derived from a proper name, are capitalized), but the book title is capitalized normally.
Chapter in multivolume edited book	[#] W. E. Hart, *A stationary point convergence theory of evolutionary algorithms*, in *Foundations of Genetic Algorithms 4*, R. K. Belew and M. D. Vose, eds., Morgan Kaufmann, San Francisco, 1997, pp. 127–134.

Software		[#] T. G. Kolda et al., *APPSPACK (Asynchronous Parallel Pattern Search Package)*; ver. 5.0.1, 2007. Available at http://software.sandia.gov/appspack/version5.0/pageDownloads.html. [#] *Windows Server 2008 R2*; ver. 6.1. Microsoft, Redmond, WA, 2009. Available at http://www.microsoft.com/windowsserver2008/en/us/default.aspx. ► When there is no author, as with this Microsoft program, alphabetize by its title.

Now, let's turn to the AMS *Bulletin* style. A few general points:

- To repeat an author's name, use three em dashes instead of the name. But do so only if *all* authors are the same.
- Capitalize only the first word (and proper nouns) for *article* titles. For book and journal titles, on the other hand, capitalize all important words; journal titles are also abbreviated.
- When the place of publication is contained in the publisher's name and is well known, then omit the place-name. Examples: Oxford UP, Cambridge UP, Princeton UP, and U Chicago P.
- To differentiate publications by the same author, include numbers after the initials. For example, assume you are citing one article published by J. Holt in 2002 and another in 2004. You could label them as [Ho2] and [Ho4], or as [Ho02] and [Ho04].
- To denote unpublished articles, you may add an asterisk if you wish, such as [Hop98*], but that is optional.

It may be helpful to see these AMS *Bulletin* citations used in an article text. Here are a couple of examples:

This question was posed by Pyber [Py3] and answered by Murray [Mu].
In [Bo98], uniform barriers are handled differently.

MATHEMATICS: AMS *BULLETIN* STYLE (ALPHABETICAL ORDER)

Journal article	[LePe07]	D.K. Levine and W. Pesendorfer: *The evolution of cooperation through imitation*, Games Econ. Behav. **58** (2007), 293–315. ► Initials such as D.K. have no spaces between them.

▸ Articles and chapters are capitalized in sentence style. Titles of books and journals, on the other hand, are capitalized normally. Journal titles are abbreviated and not italicized.

▸ Volume or issue numbers are boldfaced.

[Bo05]	I.M. Bomze: *Portfolio selection via replicator dynamics and projections of indefinite estimated covariances*, Dyn. Contin. Discrete Impuls. Syst. Ser. B Appl. Algorithms **12** (2005), 527–563. MR2167616 (**2006c**:90059) ▸ There is no punctuation after the MR number. ▸ The date and letter after the MR number are in boldface.

Journal article, online	[Ha01]	M. Haiman: *Hilbert schemes, polygraphs, and the Macdonald positivity conjecture*, J. Amer. Math. Soc. **14** (2001), 941–1006. Available at http://www.ams.org/jams/2001-14-04/S0894-0347-01-00373-3/. MR1839919 (**2002c**:14008)
	[Ho03]	J. Holt: *Multiple bumping of components of deformation spaces of hyperbolic 3-manifolds*, Amer. J. Math. **125** (2003), 691–736. Available at http://muse.jhu.edu/journals/american_journal_of_mathematics/v125/125.4holt.pdf.
Preprint	[HHL]	J. Haglund, M. Haiman, and N. Loehr: *A combinatorial formula for non-symmetric Macdonald polynomials*, preprint (2006), to appear in Amer. J. of Math. Available at arXiv: math/0601693v3 [math.CO].
Other unpublished papers	[Hop96]	M.J. Hopkins: *Course note for elliptic cohomology*, unpublished notes (1996).
	[Hop98]	———: *K(1)-local E∞ ring spectra*, unpublished notes (1998).
	[Ka]	L.K. Kamenova: *Hyper-Kaehler fibrations and Hilbert schemes*, Ph.D. diss. (2006), MIT.

Book, individual author	[Cro3]	R. Cressman: *Evolutionary Dynamics and Extensive Form Games*, MIT Press, Cambridge, MA, 2003. ▶ If you are citing several works by Cressman, you could name them by their year of publication, such as [Cr07], [Cr02]; or you could number them [Cr1], [Cr2].
Book, multiple authors	[HaSe88]	J.C. Harsany and R. Selten: *A General Theory of Equilibrium Selection in Games*, MIT Press, Cambridge, MA, 1988. MR **89j**:90285
Book, multiple editions	[KVo6]	B. Korte and J. Vygen: *Combinatorial Optimization: Theory and Algorithms*, 3rd ed., Springer-Verlag, Berlin, 2006. MR2171734 (**2006d**:90001)
Book, multivolume	[Kn]	D. Knuth: *The Art of Computer Programming*, 3rd ed., vol. 4, fasc. 3: *Generating All Combinations and Partitions*, Addison-Wesley Professional, Upper Saddle River, NJ, 2005. MR2251472
Chapter in multivolume book	[Py98]	L. Pyber: *Group enumeration and where it leads us*, in *European Congress of Mathematics: Budapest July 22–26, 1996*, vol. 2, Birkhäuser, Basel, 1998. MR **99i**:20037
Book, edited	[DR98]	L.A. Dugatkin and H.K. Reeve (eds.): *Game Theory and Animal Behaviour*, Oxford UP, 1998.
	[Nao2]	J. Nash: *The Essential John Nash*, H.W. Kuhn and S. Nasar (eds.), Princeton UP, 2002. MR **2002k**:01044
Chapter in edited book	[Bo98]	I.M. Bomze: *Uniform barriers and evolutionarily stable sets*, in W. Leinfellner, E. Köhler (eds.), *Game Theory, Experience, Rationality*, Kluwer, Dordrecht, 1998, pp. 225–244. MR **2001h**:91020

Book, online	[PU1]	F. Przytycki and M. Urbanski: *Fractals in the Plane—The Ergodic Theory Methods.* Available at http://www.math.unt.edu/~urbanski, to appear in Cambridge UP.

> ▸ Some authors add an asterisk to denote unpublished works, for example: [PU1*]. The number 1 indicates that there are other cited books by the same coauthors, such as PU2.

TEXT STYLE IN MATHEMATICS

Finally, all math papers (regardless of their citation format) have special rules governing the way to present standard terms such as theorems and proofs, as well as the way to present the text following these terms.

Mathematical term	Proper format for this term	Text after the term
theorem	THEOREM or Theorem	*Italicized*
lemma	LEMMA or Lemma	*Italicized*
corollary	COROLLARY or Corollary	*Italicized*
proof	*Proof*	Standard, no italics
definition	*Definition*	Standard, no italics
note	*Note*	Standard, no italics
remark	*Remark*	Standard, no italics
observation	*Observation*	Standard, no italics
example	*Example*	Standard, no italics

For more details, see Ellen Swanson, *Mathematics into Type,* updated by Arlene O'Sean and Antoinette Schleyer (Providence, RI: American Mathematical Society, 1999). *The Chicago Manual of Style,* chapter 12, provides an alternative guide to formatting. Either is fine as long as you are consistent.

COMPUTER SCIENCE: CITING SOURCE CODE IN PROGRAMMING

Besides citing articles and texts, you should cite others' computer code and algorithms whenever you incorporate them in your own programs. Follow the same principles you do in papers: openly acknowledge the work of others, and tell your readers where they can find it. That can be done easily in the comment section. Say who wrote the code segment you are using, the version or date it was written, where to find it, and the date you incorporated it. Be clear about where the borrowed material begins and ends, and explain what changes, if any, you made to it.

There is one exception to this citation requirement. If an algorithm is common knowledge, you don't have to cite it.

IEEE CITATIONS IN ENGINEERING

Engineers use three citation formats. Some use APA, described in chapter 5. Most prefer a format designed by one of two professional associations, the Institute of Electrical and Electronics Engineers (IEEE, pronounced "*I* triple *E*") or the American Society of Civil Engineers. The citations in this section are based on the latest *IEEE Editorial Style Manual,* published online at http://www.ieee.org/. The next section explains ASCE citations.

The IEEE publishes hundreds of journals and conference proceedings, and not just in electrical engineering and electronics. They also publish in computer science, bioengineering, civil engineering, aerospace engineering, and most of the other engineering disciplines. Still, if you're not sure IEEE is the style you should follow, consult your professor or teaching assistant.

Most IEEE journals use numbered citations in the text and the reference list. This system is similar to the one used in medicine (see chapter 8) and physics (see chapter 10). Items appear in the numbered reference list in the order they appear in the text, *not* in alphabetical order. Numbers in the text and in the reference list use brackets: [99]. The reference list uses a hanging indent to make it easier to find the numbers.

The numbers in text are treated just like any other information in brackets: according to Carmine [18]. To refer to more than one source, use commas or hyphens: in the earlier studies [3], [22]–[24]. Unlike other numbered systems, IEEE allows you to include a page number, a numbered equation, or other item along with the numbered reference: [23, pp. 18–23], [24, Fig. 13]. Equation numbers are usually in parentheses, no matter where they appear: [24, eq. (22)]. You should already know how to abbreviate page (*p.,* pl. *pp.*) and equation (*eq.,* pl. *eqs.*); for everything else, consult a dictionary. If you can't find an abbreviation, spell it out.

In the reference list itself, abbreviate authors' first names. If a reference has many authors, include them all. Capitalize titles of articles, papers, and the like as if they were sentences—only the first word and any proper names. Capitalize titles of books and periodicals normally. For journal titles, use abbreviations. For IEEE publications, you can find most of these

abbreviations in the *IEEE Editorial Style Manual* available through IEEE
.org. For anything else, consult the PubMed journals database available at
http://www.ncbi.nlm.nih.gov/journals.

IEEE (ENGINEERING): REFERENCE LIST

Journal
article, print
or online

[1] C. Koehler and T. Wischgoll, "Knowledge-assisted
reconstruction of the human rib cage and lungs," *IEEE Comput. Graph. Appl.*, vol. 30, pp. 17–29, Jan.–Feb. 2010,
doi:10.1109/MCG.2010.12.

[2] S. Samper, P.-A. Adragna, H. Favreliere, and M. Pillet,
"Modeling of 2D and 3D assemblies taking into account form
errors of plane surfaces," *J. Comput. Inf. Sci. Eng.*, vol. 9, no.
4, 041005, Dec. 2009, doi:10.1115/1.3249575.

▸ Use abbreviations for volume, page, and month (except for May,
June, and July).

▸ IEEE prefers listing the month of publication rather than the
issue number, if possible; you can also drop the issue number
for consecutively paginated volumes (i.e., most journals in the
sciences). But it's always okay to include it.

▸ Some online-only articles will not have page numbers. In the
Samper et al. example, 041005 is the "citation identifier" used by
the *Journal of Computing and Information Science in Engineering*
in place of page numbers.

▸ For citing online sources, the IEEE follows APA. If a DOI is
available—even if you read the article on paper—include it. If
you don't see a DOI, list the URL (usually, the address in your
browser's location bar) instead. DOI stands for Digital Object
Identifier. Pasting a DOI into a DOI resolver (available from
CrossRef.org) will direct you to the article—wherever it is posted.

Unpublished
article or
paper

[#] Q.-Y. Xu, X. Li, C.-Q. Xu, and W.-P. Huang, "Modulation
crosstalk and reduction in distributed feedback laser diode
and monitor photodiode monolithically integrated optical
transceivers," *IEEE J. Quantum Electron.*, to be published.

▸ If an article has been accepted for publication, use "to be published." If it has been submitted but not yet accepted, omit the
name of any journal and say "submitted for publication" following
the title of the unpublished article.

[#] N. S. Cheruvu, "Nanocrystalline coatings for ultra super-
critical boiler and turbine components," presented at the 4th
Int. Conf. on Surfaces, Coatings and Nanostructured Materials (NANOSMAT), Rome, Italy, Oct. 2009.

▶ Abbreviate *conference* and words like *national* or *international*, but, for the most part, spell out the name of the event.

Published conference proceedings	[#] L. Xie and Z. Mo, "Decision system of urban rail transit line construction sequence," in *Proc. 2nd Int. Conf. Transportation Engineering*, Chengdu, China, July 25–27, 2009, pp. 820–825. ▶ The IEEE manual insists on page numbers. ▶ The manual also lists a few terms to abbreviate, including those above. The full title for the proceedings in the example is *Proceedings of the Second International Conference on Transportation Engineering* (notice that prepositions and articles drop out).

Book, one author	[#] G. Rizzoni, *Fundamentals of Electrical Engineering*. Dubuque, IA: McGraw-Hill, 2009, p. 92. ▶ Include page number(s) unless the citation is to the whole book.

Book, multiple authors	[#] L. T. Biegler, I. E. Grossmann, and A. W. Westerberg, *Systematic Methods of Chemical Process Design*. Upper Saddle River, NJ: Prentice Hall, 1997. ▶ IEEE says to list all authors. If this gets to be impractical, list only the first and add "et al." Example: L. T. Biegler et al., *Systematic Methods . . .*

Book, multiple editions	[#] B. K. Donaldson, *Analysis of Aircraft Structures: An Introduction* (Cambridge Aerospace Series 24), 2nd ed. New York: Cambridge Univ. Press, 2008.

Book, multivolume	[#] J.-P. Françoise, G. L. Naber, and T. S. Tsun, Eds., *Encyclopedia of Mathematical Physics*, 5 vols. San Diego: Academic Press/Elsevier, 2006. ▶ IEEE capitalizes the abbreviations for *editor* (Ed.) and *editors* (Eds). They do seem to like their capital *E*s.

Chapter in book	[#] A. Wada, Y. Huang, and V. Bertero, "Innovative strategies in earthquake engineering," in *Earthquake Engineering: From Engineering Seismology to Performance-Based Engineering*, Y. Bozorgnia and V. Bertero, Eds. Boca Raton, FL: CRC Press, 2004, pp. 637–675.

Book, online	[#] D. Haskell, A. Pillay, and C. Steinhorn, Eds., *Model Theory, Algebra, and Geometry* (MSRI Publications 39) [Online], http://www.msri.org/publications/books/Book39/contents.html.

▶ For Internet sources, you might omit "Online," since that's clear from the URL. To cite a Kindle book or other electronic edition, put that in the brackets instead of "Online" (e.g., [Kindle version]).

Patent	[#] P. Vinh, L. Yu, and M. J. Vainikka, "Power control of packet data transmission in cellular network," U.S. Patent 7,653,857, Jan. 26, 2010.

ASCE CITATIONS IN ENGINEERING

Unlike the IEEE, the American Society of Civil Engineers prefers the author-date style for its books and journals authors. This style is similar to APA (chapter 5). The differences are (what else?) in the details. A few of these details can be found on the ASCE website (at http://pubs.asce.org/authors/journal/).

The author-date style uses an alphabetical reference list. Each entry in the reference list must be mentioned in the text, and vice versa. Let's start with a few examples:

Brenner, B. (2006). "Bringing out the inner civil engineer." *Don't throw this away! The civil engineering life,* ASCE Press, Reston, Va., 23–25.

Brenner, B. (2009a). *Bridginess: More of the civil engineering life,* ASCE Press, Reston, Va.

Brenner, B. (2009b). "Infrastructure at the end." *Leadersh. Manage. Eng.* 9(4), 205–206.

Compare these if you'd like with the examples at the beginning of chapter 5 (featuring the eminent author C. Lipson). Like APA, ASCE uses author's initials and puts the date in parentheses. Titles by the same author are listed in chronological order; two titles by the same author in the same year are alphabetized by title and carry letters after the date.

Unlike APA, ASCE prefers quotation marks around article and chapter titles. And, like most science publishers, they use abbreviations for journal titles. Where to find these? If it's not listed along with the journal article, search the PubMed journals database available at http://www.ncbi.nlm .nih.gov/journals. (Just remember to add periods to the ends of abbreviated elements in the title.)

In text, cite the author and year, with no intervening comma: (Brenner 2009b). If you need to include a page number, use a comma; separate two references with a semicolon: (Brenner 2006, p. 88; Brenner 2009a). ASCE journals often differ in these details. Mainly, you need to worry about being consistent. If you happen to be writing for a particular journal, look at a few recent articles in that journal and style your references accordingly. If you can't find a particular type of example and it isn't listed below, look at chapter 5 for a model and adapt that.

For the sake of comparison, the examples in the table that follows cite many of the same sources as those in the IEEE section above.

ASCE (ENGINEERING): REFERENCE LIST

Journal article, print or online	Koehler, C., and Wischgoll, T. (2010). "Knowledge-assisted reconstruction of the human rib cage and lungs." *IEEE Comput. Graph. Appl.* 30(1), 17–29, doi:10.1109/MCG .2010.12.
	Samper, S., Adragna, P.-A., Favreliere, H., and Pillet, M. (2009). "Modeling of 2D and 3D assemblies taking into account form errors of plane surfaces." *J. Comput. Inf. Sci. Eng.* 9(4), 041005, doi:10.1115/1.3249575.

- ▸ ASCE wants you to list volume and issue number instead of month or season.
- ▸ Some online-only articles will not have page numbers. In the Samper et al. example, 041005 is the "citation identifier" used by the *Journal of Computing and Information Science in Engineering* in place of page numbers.
- ▸ The ASCE online guide for authors doesn't give much advice for citing online sources. Because their system is close to that of APA, follow APA (unless your professor says otherwise). If a DOI is available—even if you read the article on paper—include it. If you don't see a DOI, list the URL (usually, the address in your browser's location bar) instead. DOI stands for Digital Object Identifier. Pasting a DOI into a DOI resolver (available from CrossRef.org) will direct you to the article—wherever it is posted.

Unpublished article or paper	Xu, Q.-Y., Li, X., Xu, C.-Q., and Huang, W.-P. (2010). "Modulation crosstalk and reduction in distributed feedback laser diode and monitor photodiode monolithically integrated optical transceivers." *IEEE J. Quantum Electron.* 46(3), 323–331, advance online publication, Jan. 26, doi:10.1109/JQE.2009.2033611.

▶ In the references, list all authors. In text, if there are three or more, cite only the first, followed by "et al.": (Xu et al. 2010).

▶ The Xu et al. article was published online on January 26, 2010—ahead of the March issue (vol. 46, no. 3). If you cite the advance version, it's best to say so. (I've modeled this advice on APA.)

▶ ASCE advises against citing unpublished articles, papers, reports, and the like in the reference list. But you can cite them in text: According to A. Stradivari (unpublished manuscript, January 2010) . . .

Published conference proceedings	Xie, L., and Mo, Z. (2009). "Decision system of urban rail transit line construction sequence." *Proc., 2nd Int. Conf. on Transportation Engineering*, Southwest Jiantong University, Chengdu, China, July 25–27, doi:10.1061 /41039(345)136.

▶ Like IEEE, ASCE abbreviates titles of published proceedings. Unlike IEEE, they substitute a comma for "of the" and don't object to the preposition "on."

▶ These proceedings were also published as a book. To cite the same paper but from the book, you could list the publisher instead of the conference location—in this case, ASCE, Reston, Va. Then you'd include page numbers instead of a DOI.

Xie, L., and Mo, Z. (2009). "Decision system of urban rail transit line construction sequence." *Proc., 2nd Int. Conf. on Transportation Engineering*, ASCE, Reston, Va., 820–825.

Book, one author	Rizzoni, G. (2009). *Fundamentals of electrical engineering.* McGraw-Hill, Dubuque, Iowa.

▶ ASCE recommends "traditional" state abbreviations rather than postal codes (e.g., Pa. rather than PA). There is no traditional abbreviation for Iowa. To find the right one, use a dictionary or consult *The Chicago Manual of Style.*

Book, multiple authors	Biegler, L. T., Grossmann, I. E., and Westerberg, A. W. (1997). *Systematic methods of chemical process design*. Prentice Hall, Upper Saddle River, N.J. ▸ List all authors in the reference list. In text, if there are three or more, list the first and add "et al.": (Biegler et al. 1997).
Book, multiple editions	Donaldson, B. K. (2008). *Analysis of aircraft structures: An introduction*, 2nd ed., Cambridge Aerospace Series 24, Cambridge Univ. Press, New York, N.Y.
Book, multivolume	Françoise, J.-P., Naber, G. L., and Tsun, T. S., eds. (2006). *Encyclopedia of mathematical physics*, 5 vols., Academic Press/Elsevier, San Diego, Calif.
Chapter in book	Wada, A., Huang, Y., and Bertero, V. (2004). "Innovative strategies in earthquake engineering." *Earthquake engineering: From engineering seismology to performance-based engineering*, Y. Bozorgnia and V. Bertero, eds., CRC Press, Boca Raton, Fla., 637–675.
Book, online	Haskell, D., Pillay, A., and Steinhorn, C., eds. (2000). *Model theory, algebra, and geometry* (Online), MSRI Publications 39, http://www.msri.org/publications/books/Book39/contents.html. ▸ For Internet sources, you might omit "Online," since that's clear from the URL. To cite a Kindle book or other electronic edition, put that in the parentheses instead of "Online"—e.g., (Kindle version).
Patent	Vinh, P., Yu, L., and Vainikka, M. J. (2010). "Power control of packet data transmission in cellular network," U.S. Patent 7,653,857, Jan. 26.

12 FAQS ABOUT *ALL* REFERENCE STYLES

WHAT SHOULD YOU CITE?

Do I need to cite everything I use in the paper?
Pretty much. Cite anything you rely on for data or authoritative opinions. Cite both quotes and paraphrases. Cite personal communications such as e-mails, interviews, or conversations with professors if you rely on them for your paper. If you rely heavily on any single source, make that clear, either with multiple citations or with somewhat fewer citations plus a clear statement that you are relying on a particular source for a particular topic.

There is one exception. Don't cite sources for facts that are well-known to your audience. It's overkill to cite any authorities for the signing of the Declaration of Independence on July 4, 1776. There will be time enough to footnote them when you start discussing the politics of the Continental Congress.

How many citations does a paper have, anyway?
It varies and there is no exact number, but a couple per page is common in well-researched papers. More is fine. If there are no citations for several pages in a row, something's probably wrong. Most likely, you just forgot to include them. You need to go back and fix the problem.

How many different sources should I use?
That depends on how complicated your subject is, how intensively you've studied it, and how long your paper is. If it is a complex subject or one that is debated intensely, you'll need to reflect that with multiple sources—some to present facts, some to cover different sides of the issue. On the other hand, if it's a short paper on a straightforward topic, you might need only a couple of sources. If you are unsure, ask what your professor expects for your topic. While you're talking, you might also ask about the best sources to use.

In any case, don't base longer, more complex papers on two or three sources, even if they are very good ones. Your paper should be more than a gloss on others' work (unless it is specifically an analysis of that scholar's work). It should be an original work that stands on its own. Use a variety of sources and make sure they include a range of opinions on any controversial topic.

You certainly don't need to agree with all sides. You are not made of rubber. But, at least for longer papers and hotly debated topics, you need to show that you have read different views, wrestled with varied ideas, and responded to the most important points.

By the way, your notes can be negative citations, as well as positive. You are welcome to disagree openly with a source, or you can simply say, "For an alternative view, see . . ."

WHAT GOES IN A CITATION?

Can I include discussion or analysis in notes?

Yes, for most styles, *except in the sciences.* Footnotes or endnotes are fine spots to add brief insights that bear on your paper topic but would distract from your narrative if they were included in the text. Just remember you still need to edit these discursive notes, just as you do the rest of your writing. And don't let them become a major focus of your writing effort. The text is the main event.

If you use in-text citations such as (Tarcov 2010) and want to add some explanatory notes, you'll have to add them as a special set of citations. They are usually marked with a superscript number, such as (Tarcov 2010).[3] In this case, note 3 would be the explanatory text.

If you are writing in the sciences and already using superscripts for the citation-sequence system, you're better off avoiding explanatory notes entirely. If you really need to include one or two, mark them with an asterisk or other symbol. In this system, you cannot use numbered citations for anything except references.

I sometimes use articles from *Time* or *Newsweek*. Should they be cited like journal articles or newspaper articles?

That depends on how long and how significant the articles are. Short pieces in newsweeklies are usually treated like newspaper articles. You can include the author, but you don't have to. Either way, short articles are not usually included in the bibliography. Major articles with author bylines are treated more like journal articles and are included in the bibliography.

Some styles, notably Chicago-style references, use shortened citations after the first citation for an item. What's the best way to shorten a title? There are some standard ways. One is to use only the author's last name: Strunk and White instead of William Strunk Jr. and E. B. White. You also drop the initial article in the title and any other needless words. *The Elements of Style* becomes *Elements of Style*. Drop the edition number and all publishing information, such as the publisher's name. For articles, drop the journal title and volume. So:

Long form   99 William Strunk Jr. and E. B. White, *The Elements of Style,* 4th ed. (New York: Longman, 2000), 12.
100 Stefan Elbe, "HIV/AIDS and the Changing Landscape of War in Africa," *International Security* 27 (Fall 2002): 159–77.

Short form   199 Strunk and White, *Elements of Style,* 12.
200 Elbe, "HIV/AIDS," 162.

The shortened title for Elbe's work might be confusing if your paper dealt mainly with HIV/AIDS and was filled with similar citations. For clarity, you might decide on an alternative short title such as "Landscape of War."

If the title has two parts, put on your surgical gloves and remove the colon (and everything that follows it).

Long form   99 Robert A. Kaster, *Guardians of Language: The Grammarian and Society in Late Antiquity* (Berkeley: University of California Press, 1988).
100 Kenneth Shultz and Barry Weingast, "The Democratic Advantage: Institutional Foundations of Financial Power in International Competition," *International Organization* 57 (Winter 2003): 3–42.

Short form   199 Kaster, *Guardians of Language.*
200 Shultz and Weingast, "Democratic Advantage."

You might need to shorten a title by identifying a few key words. Take Francis Robinson, ed., *Cambridge Illustrated History of the Islamic World.* There is no single right way to shorten this, but the best title is probably: Robinson, *History of Islamic World.* (Note that Robinson is simply listed as the author; his title as editor is dropped.)

In the first full note, you can also tell readers how you will shorten a title. After giving the full title for Senate Banking Committee hearings on terrorist money laundering, for instance, you might say: (subsequently called "2004 Senate hearings").

What about citing a work I've found in someone else's notes? Do I need to cite the place where I discovered the work?

This issue comes up all the time because it's one of the most important ways we learn about other works and other ideas. Reading a book by E. L. Jones, for example, you find an interesting citation to Adam Smith. As it turns out, you are more interested in Smith's point than in Jones's commentary, so you decide to cite Smith. That's fine—you can certainly cite Smith—but how should you handle it?

There's a choice. One way is to follow the paper trail from Jones's note to Adam Smith's text, read the relevant part, and simply cite it, with no reference at all to Jones. That's completely legitimate for books like Smith's that are well known in their field. You are likely to come across such works in your normal research, and you don't need to cite Jones as the guide who sent you there. To do that honestly, though, you have to go to Smith and read the relevant parts.

The rule is simple: *Cite only texts you have actually used and would have found in the normal course of your research,* not obscure texts used by someone else or works you know about only secondhand. You don't have to read several hundred pages of Adam Smith. You do have to read the relevant pages in Smith—the ones you cite. Remember the basic principle: *When you say you did the work yourself, you actually did it.*

Alternatively, if you don't have time to read Smith yourself (or if the work is written in a language you cannot read), you can cite the text this way: "Smith, *Wealth of Nations,* 123, as discussed in Jones, *The European Miracle.*" Normally, you don't need to cite the page in Jones, but you can if you wish. An in-text citation would look different but accomplish the same thing: (Smith 123, qtd. in Jones).

This alternative is completely honest, too. You are referencing Smith's point but saying you found it in Jones. This follows another equally important principle: *When you rely on someone else's work, you cite it.* In this case, you are relying on Jones, not Smith himself, as your source for Smith's point.

Follow the same rule if Jones leads you to a work that is unusual or obscure *to you,* a work you discovered only because Jones did the detailed research, found it, and told you about it. For example, one of Jones's citations is to a 1668 book by Paul Rycaut, entitled *The Present State of the Ottoman Empire.* I'm not an expert on the Ottoman Empire and certainly would not have discovered that book myself. Frankly, I'd never even heard of it until Jones mentioned it. So I'd cite it as (Rycaut 54, cited in Jones).

I can do that without going to the Rycaut book. On the other hand, if I were a student of Ottoman history and Jones had simply reminded me of Rycaut's work, I could cite it directly. To do that honestly, however, I would need to go to the Rycaut volume and read the relevant passage.

Some scholars, unfortunately, sneak around this practice. They don't give credit where credit is due. They simply cite Rycaut, even if they've never heard of him before, or they cite Smith, even if they haven't read the passage. One result (and it really happens!) could be that Jones made a mistake in his citation and the next scholar repeated the error. It's really a twofold blunder: an incorrect footnote and a false assertion that the writer used Smith as a source.

The specific rules here are less important than the basic concepts:

- Cite only texts you found in the normal course of your research and have actually used.
- Cite all your sources openly and honestly.

Follow these and you'll do just fine.

BIBLIOGRAPHY

Do I need to have a bibliography?

Yes, for all styles *except* complete Chicago notes. If you use complete Chicago citations, not the short versions, the first note for each item gives readers complete information, including the title and publisher, so you don't need a bibliography. (You are welcome to include a bibliography if you use Chicago style, but you don't have to, unless your professor requires it.)

All other styles require a bibliography for a simple reason. The notes themselves are too brief to describe the sources fully.

Should my bibliography include the general background reading I did for the paper?

The answer depends on how much you relied on a particular reading and which reference style you use. MLA, APA, and science bibliographies include only the works you have actually cited. Chicago-style bibliographies are more flexible and can include works you haven't cited in a note.

My advice is this: If a work was really useful to you, then check to make sure you have acknowledged that debt somewhere with a citation. After you've cited it once, the work will appear in your bibliography, regardless of which style you use. If a particular background reading wasn't important in your research, don't worry about citing it.

Does the bibliography raise any questions about my work?
Yes, readers will scan your bibliography to see what kinds of sources you used and whether they are the best ones. There are five problems to watch out for:

- Old, out-of-date works
- Bias in the overall bibliography
- Omission of major works in your subject
- Reliance on poor or weak sources
- Excessive reliance on one or two sources

These are not really problems with the bibliography, as such. They are problems with the text that become apparent by looking at the bibliography.

Old sources are great for some purposes but antiquated for others. Many consider Gibbon's *Decline and Fall of the Roman Empire* the greatest historical work ever written. But no one today would use it as a major secondary source on Rome or Byzantium. Too much impressive research has been completed in the two centuries since Gibbon wrote. So, if you were writing about current views of Byzantium or ancient Rome, *Decline and Fall* would be out-of-date. Relying on it would cast a shadow on your research. On the other hand, if you were writing about great historical works, eighteenth-century perspectives, or changing views about Byzantium, using Gibbon would be perfectly appropriate, perhaps essential.

"Old" means different things in different fields. A work published ten or fifteen years ago might be reasonably current in history, literature, and some areas of mathematics, depending on how fast those fields are changing. For a discipline moving at warp speed like genetics, an article might be out-of-date within a year. A paper in molecular genetics filled with citations from 2003 or even 2007 would cast serious doubt on the entire project. Whatever your field, you should rely on the best works and make sure they have not been superseded by newer, better research.

Bias, omission of key works, and overreliance on a few sources reveal other problems.[1] Bias means you have looked at only one side of a multifaceted issue. Your bibliography might indicate bias if it lists readings on only one side of a contested issue. Omitting an authoritative work not

---

1. Ralph Berry, *The Research Project: How to Write It* (London: Routledge, 2000), 108–9.

only impoverishes your work; it leaves readers wondering if you studied the topic carefully.

The remedy for all these problems is the same. For longer, more complex papers, at least, you need to read a variety of major works in your subject and indicate that with citations.

However long (or short!) your paper, make sure your sources are considered solid and reliable. Your professors and teaching assistants can really help here. They know the literature and should be valuable guides.

QUOTATIONS

I am using a quotation that contains a second quote within it. How do I handle the citation?
Let's say your paper includes the following sentence:

> According to David M. Kennedy, Roosevelt began his new presidency "by reassuring his countrymen that 'this great nation will endure as it has endured, will revive and will prosper. . . . The only thing we have to fear . . . is fear itself.'"

Of course, you'll cite Kennedy, but do you need to cite *his* source for the Roosevelt quote? No. It's not required. In some cases, however, your readers will benefit from a little extra information about the quote within a quote. You can easily do that in your footnote or endnote:

99 Kennedy, *Freedom from Fear,* 134. The Roosevelt quote comes from his 1933 inaugural address.

I am quoting from some Spanish and French books and doing the translations myself. How should I handle the citations?
Just include the words "my translation" immediately after the quote or in the citation. You don't need to do this each time. After the first quotation, you can tell your readers that you are translating all quotes yourself. Then cite the foreign-language text you are using.

In some papers, you might want to include quotes in both the original and translation. That's fine. Either the translation or the original can come first; the other follows in parentheses or brackets. For instance:

> In Madame Pompadour's famous phrase, "Après nous, le déluge." (After us, the flood.) As it turned out, she was right.

ELECTRONIC MATERIALS AND MICROFILM

I was reading a blog and found some information I want to cite. But the blog is not the original source. It links to some website for the information. Which one should I cite?
It's best to cite the location where the information originated. In this case, that's the website rather than the blog. To cite the web page honestly, however, you actually need to go there and check it out.

Unfortunately, you can't always find the original source. One blog links to another, which links to a third, and you can't figure out who in this daisy chain originated the information. What should you do, then? First, if you cannot find the original source, cite the best source you have and note that it says the information originates elsewhere (or does not indicate its source for the information). "Blog A, based on information from website B." Second, if you cannot find the original source, be very careful about using the information at all. You don't have a good way to tell fact from urban legend.

These rules are similar to those for print sources. The media may be new, but the rules are not. Cite the source that originates the information, not a secondary source, if you can. And remember that, to cite any source directly, you *must* go there and check out the information firsthand. You cannot just copy a citation from someone else.

Some citations list "microfilm." Others list "microform" or "microfiche." What's the difference? Do I need to mention any of them in my citations?
They are all tiny photographic images, read with magnifying tools. Libraries use these formats to save money and storage space for large document collections. *All* these images are called *microforms,* no matter what material they are stored on. When they are stored on reels of film, they're called *microfilm.* When they are stored on plastic sheets or cards, they're called *microfiche.*

When you use materials that have been photographically reduced like this, you should say so in the citation, just as you do for websites or electronic information. (If the microforms simply reproduce printed material exactly, some citation styles allow you to cite the printed material directly. But you are always safe if you mention that you read it on microfilm or microfiche. The same is true for citing print items that are reproduced electronically.)

The URL I'm citing is long and needs to go on two lines. How do I handle the line break?

Here's the technical answer. If the URL takes up more than one line, break *after* a

- colon and double slash

break *before* a

- slash
- period
- comma
- question mark
- tilde (~)
- ampersand (&)
- hyphen
- underline
- number sign

Here are some examples:

Full URL	http://www.charleslipson.com/index.htm
Break before slash	http://www.charleslipson.com /index.htm
Break before other punctuation	http://www.charleslipson .com/index.htm

These "break rules" apply to all citation styles.

There's a rationale for these rules. Some URLs end in a slash; break before the slash to show that the URL continues on the next line. By a similar logic, if periods, commas, or hyphens come at the end of a line, they might be mistaken for punctuation marks. By contrast, when they come at the beginning of a line, they are clearly part of the URL. To avoid confusion, don't add hyphens to break long words in the URL.

You can produce such breaks in a number of ways. One is to insert a line break by pressing the shift-enter keys simultaneously in Word or the shift-return keys on a Mac. Alternatively, you can insert a space in the URL so your word-processing program automatically wraps the URL onto the next line. (Without such a space, the word processor might force the entire URL onto its own line, then—if it's really long—break it either at a hyphen or randomly at the end of the line.) A third way—if you know how—is to insert an optional break using your word processor's special characters function.

Even though you are technically allowed to break URLs before periods, commas, and hyphens, I try to avoid such breaks because these punctuation marks are easy to overlook at the beginning of a line and might confuse readers. Instead, I usually break only before a slash (or after a double slash), and then only when I am printing the final version of the paper. When I'm sending it electronically, I try to avoid breaks altogether. That way, the recipient will have "live" hyperlinks to click on.

Isn't there a computer program that can handle all these citation issues for me?

Yes and no. There are some excellent computer programs that can capture information from library catalogs and other online databases and format it for you in whatever citation style you want.

It sounds easy, but these programs have significant limitations. They work best with books and recent journal articles, where the source information is usually standardized and available for download. They are less helpful when you want to cite a source that's older or more unusual— perhaps a letter in a physical archive, a video on YouTube, a painting in a gallery, or an article in a long-defunct newspaper. There simply isn't a database with full information about these items.

These differences in source materials mean that citation software is most useful in the physical and biological sciences and the quantitative social sciences. It is less useful in the humanities and interpretative social sciences, where the sources are more diverse and therefore less likely to be encoded in standard databases.

Let me fill in some details. Programs like EndNote, RefWorks, and Zotero allow you to build libraries of source citations and plug them directly into your papers. You can pick whatever citation style you want, and you can easily change from one citation style to another. The programs are designed to work with standardized databases, although you can type in the information if it's not available online.

The good news is that these databases are increasingly common. Most library catalogs and other bibliographic databases are designed so you can download citations directly into the software, and more and more publishers are following suit with their online catalogs. But, as with any new program, you'll need to spend some time learning the ins and outs.

This learning process may take longer in the humanities and social sciences, where the range of sources means you'll need to do some extra work. Instead of just pushing a button and downloading your data, you'll often need to pull up a blank record and enter the data from scratch. These records have a specific structure for entering data. You'll need to follow that structure, enter the information carefully, avoid typos, and use any punctuation required by the program. In one program I use, for instance, multiple authors must be separated by a semicolon. Not a comma. A semicolon.

Later, when you insert citations into your papers, it's wise to double-check the output and make sure it's accurate. That applies to the materials you've downloaded from databases, too. If the original material was encoded incorrectly, the citations will show it. I know. I once printed out a citation for a recent edition of Plato's work. It said the editor was Plato's coauthor. Actually, Plato did not have coauthors, and if he did, he would have had to wait 2,500 years for this one. I returned to the software and restored Plato to his rightful place as a single (and singular) author.

Before you start using the software, it helps to know which citation style you'll be using for your papers. It's not essential, but it helps. You'll know what to enter for each type of source, and you'll know what you can skip (each record will have spaces for countless details). You might even be able to catch what the software has missed and fix it.

One final point. If you are using your university's citation software and plan to continue your studies, perhaps at another university, you should check with your university and learn about exporting your citation library. If your citation data is stored on the university's servers, you'll need to make arrangements to move it. After you spent all that time building your library, you'll want to keep it with you as you continue your education.

Over time, the software is sure to get better and better and the databases more comprehensive. But right now, it's still a mixed bag.

Tips on citing web pages: As you take notes, write down the

- URL for the website or web page (copy and paste to avoid errors)
- Name or description of the page or site
- Date you accessed it

Writing the name or description of a website is useful because if the URL changes (as they sometimes do), you still can find it by searching.

As for the access date, some citation styles, such as MLA and AMA, require it. Others, such as *The Chicago Manual of Style* and APA, make it optional. They tell you to include it only when it's relevant, such as for frequently updated sources (think *Wikipedia*).

If sites are particularly useful, add them to your "favorites" list (i.e., bookmark them). If you add several sites for a paper, create a new category (or folder) named for the paper and drop the URLs into that. A folder will gather the sites in a single location and keep them from getting lost in your long list of favorites.

Finally, whenever you cite something that looks as if it is likely to change or disappear sometime tomorrow or even next year, it is a good idea to print it out and save a copy of it. This holds for such things as blog entries, comments on social networking sites, articles in wikis, and for any website—including online newspapers. Anything that might be redesigned, deleted, discontinued, or subtly (or not so subtly) altered without notice. If you're citing something like the online version of an article in a scholarly journal, however, you probably don't need to save a copy. Most journals have pretty strict rules about making and posting revisions, and they usually do a good job of archiving past issues.

SCIENCE CITATIONS

In the sciences, some citations include terms like DOI and PMID. What are they? Do I need to include them in my citations?
They identify articles within large electronic databases. Just like other parts of your citations, these unique IDs help readers locate articles and data you have used. In fact, you may use them yourself to return to an article for more research.

Not every scientific journal includes them in citations or lists them for its own articles. Some do; some don't. (Many use them "under the hood," to allow links to and from references in the online versions of their articles.) My advice: When you do research, write the numbers down and consider including them in your own citations. They appear at the very end of each citation, right after the pagination and URL.

What do the various letters mean? DOI stands for Digital Object Identifier. It's an international system for identifying and exchanging intellectual property on the web and other networks. Like a URL, it can be used to locate an item (e.g., by pasting it into the DOI resolver available from CrossRef.org). Unlike a URL, it remains the same, even if the item is moved to a new location. Some style guides advise listing DOIs rather than URLs when they're available (Chicago, APA, AMA).

PMID appears in many medical and biological journals. It stands for PubMed Identifier. The PubMed database includes virtually all biomedical journals plus some preprints. It is available online at http://www.ncbi.nlm.nih.gov/pubmed/ and has a tutorial for new users. This invaluable database was developed by the National Center for Biotechnology Information at the National Library of Medicine.

Other specialized fields have their own electronic identifiers. MR, for example, refers to articles in the Mathematical Reviews database. Physics has identifying numbers for preprints (prepublication articles), which classifies them by subfield.

You are not required to list any of these electronic identifiers in your citations, but doing so may help you and your readers.

In the sciences, I'm supposed to abbreviate journal titles. Where do I find these abbreviations?
The easiest way is to look at the first page of the article you are citing. It usually includes the abbreviation and often the full citation for the article. You can also go to various websites assembled by reference librarians, listing journal abbreviations in many fields. One useful resource is "All That JAS: Journal Abbreviation Sources," compiled by Gerry McKiernan, Science and Technology Librarian and Bibliographer at Iowa State, and available at http://www.abbreviations.com/jas.asp. And there's always the National Library of Medicine's publically accessible database of tens of thousands of journals, available at http://www.ncbi.nlm.nih.gov/journals—and by no means limited to medical titles.

INDEX

in AIP and astrophysics/astronomy
styles, 176
in APA style, 106–7
in Chicago style, 28–29
in MLA style, 74–75
DOIs (Digital Object Identifiers), rules
for, 205–6
in AAA style, 131
in AIP and astrophysics/astronomy
styles, 173, 175
in AMA style, 159, 164
in APA style, 103, 104
in Chicago style, 25, 30
in CSE style, 147
in IEEE and ASCE styles, 188, 191
See also URLs, access dates, and other
electronic identifiers, rules for
DVDs and CDs, citation of
in ACS style, 171
in AMA style, 163
in Chicago style, 43
in CSE style, 151, 155

e-books, citation of
in APA style, 100–101
in Chicago style, 20–21
in IEEE and ASCE styles, 190, 193
in MLA style, 69
editors, rules for names of. *See* names of
authors and other creators, rules for
education (field), citations in, 95–123
electronic identifiers, rules for. *See* URLs,
access dates, and other electronic
identifiers, rules for
e-mail, text, and instant messages and
electronic groups, citation of
in APA style, 122
in Chicago style, 58–59
in MLA style, 92
See also personal communications,
citation of
encyclopedias, citation of. *See* reference
works, citation of

endnotes, basic format of. *See* notes,
basic format of
engineering, citations in, 6, 95, 187–93
ethnography, citations in, 124–43
exhibition catalogs, citation of in AAA
style, 133–34

figures, citation of
in AAA style, 140
in APA style, 114–15
in Chicago style, 45–46
in MLA style, 84–85
films and television programs, citation of
in AAA style, 139
in APA style, 113
in Chicago style, 42–44
in MLA style, 82–83
footnotes, basic format of. *See* notes,
basic format of

government documents, citation of
in AAA style, 141
in ACS style, 170
in AMA style, 162–63
in APA style, 115–16
in Chicago style, 49–51
in CSE style, 151, 154
in MLA style, 87–88
graphs, citation of. *See* figures, citation of

hanging indents, 9–10, 17
humanities, citations in, 4, 6–11, 15–62,
63–94

IEEE style, 6, 187–90
instant messages, citation of. *See*
e-mail, text, and instant messages
and electronic groups, citation of
Internet sources, citation of. *See specific
types of sources by name*
interviews, citation of
in AAA style, 138–39
in APA style, 112